F

Kees —
To the best devil's
advocate I've met in
years!

[signature]

To my parents,
who taught me to "look up, and laugh,
and love, and lift."

First Impression, Best Impression

by Janet G. Elsea, Ph.D.

Originally published as *The Four-Minute Sell*

A Fireside Book
Published by Simon & Schuster, Inc.
New York

Designed by Wordscape, Inc.
Produced by Tilden Press, Inc.

Manufactured in the United States of America

5   7   9   10   8   6   4   Pbk.

Library of Congress Cataloging-in-Publication Data

Elsea, Janet G.
First impression, best impression.

"Originally published as The four-minute sell."
"A Fireside book."
Bibliography: p.
Includes index.
1. Success in business.   2. Communication in
management.   3. Nonverbal communication (Psychology)
I. Elsea, Janet G.   Four-minute sell. II. Title.
HF5386.E46   1985   650.1'3   85-25322
ISBN 0-671-55545-6 Pbk.

Contents

Acknowledgments

*T*here are some people whose positive imprint on my life led directly to completion of this book. I'd like to thank a few of them:

My Washington, D.C., family of friends and clients kept up the calls, food, beverage and encouragement: Brenda, Jim, Robin, Bernie, Peg, Rich, Aija, Diane, Ginny and Dr. Y.

My Arizona family, both in Phoenix and Tucson, checked in by phone and mail: Fran and the kids, Carolyn, Kristin, Gene, Muldoon, K.S.R., Tyree, Randy, Penel and Mayor Murphy.

And my own kin in California—my parents, Jim and Wilma Elsea, sister Madeline and brother Rollie: their love and support reach powerfully beyond the miles.

Joel Makower, president of Tilden Press, saw me through every word of this book and introduced me to literary agent Raphael Sagalyn. The gentle and careful prodding of Bob Bender, my editor at Simon & Schuster, led me to write in a whole new way.

Preface

*L*ate one fall evening in 1982, I received a call from my friend John May, who had an important interview the next day with a client regarding a potential six-figure contract. "I want to look and sound good," said John. "What should I wear? What can I say first to set the mood? How will I know how well I'm doing?"

I gave him some suggestions and wished him well. "Elsea," he said, "why don't you put that stuff in a book? You'd give a lot of us some ammunition we badly need out there in the cold, cruel business world."

And so I wrote this book – for John and for all the other friends and clients who have clamored for "something in writing." These business and professional people know intuitively that appearance, body language, choice of words and tone of voice are critical to selling yourself and making a good first impression. But even with all their professional degrees, expertise and experience, they simply aren't certain how to go about it. Few people are trained in interpersonal communication.

Successful managers and executives must be good communicators and salespeople, whether they are selling their products, services or ideas. Too many promising careers are sidetracked, promotions lost, customers angered or relationships destroyed because people didn't know the strategies of good personal communication. Otherwise intelligent people

1

didn't know what they looked like or sounded like when making new contacts.

This book tells you what you need to know to put together your strategy for making a positive first impression in the crucial first few minutes, when long-lasting judgments are formed. In the pages that follow, you'll learn what happens when you meet someone for the first time, including the predictable, natural sequence most people go through when meeting someone. You'll learn how to evaluate yourself — and how to evaluate others – to detect honesty, stress, fear, professionalism and other traits. You'll be asked four key questions about yourself: "What do I LOOK like?" "What do I SOUND like?" "What do I SAY?" and "How well do I LISTEN?" And you'll be given suggestions for making your part of the communication process work to enormous advantage.

The bottom line is that you will be armed with a powerful set of weapons for selling yourself and your ideas and for interpreting other people's behavior.

I have experienced and studied communication from nearly all perspectives: student, scholar, teacher, administrator, employee and business executive. This book draws on that experience: on my formal training as a Ph.D. in speech communication, on important research from the fields of communication and sociology, on actual case studies from my work with clients and on time-tested practical strategies that I've seen turn around careers and some lives.

Communication is the central act of our lives — particularly our business lives. In 1978, I founded Communications Skills, Inc., a communication consulting firm, with that fact in mind. I explain the importance of communication to clients throughout this country – at the World Bank in Washington, D.C.; at Humana, Inc., in Louisville; at Valley National Bank in Arizona; at public broadcasting stations throughout the country. In each situation, the communication strategy is essentially the same, whether you're meeting alone with a chief executive officer or giving a presentation to a group of colleagues or clients. The message you'll find throughout this book is this: communication is not the transmission of information; it is the sharing of meaning.

Doctor, lawyer, Indian chief, salesperson, job-seeker and CEO – the communication process is critical for all.

Chapter One
The First Four Minutes

Chapter One

The First Four Minutes

*T*he fortune cookie is right. You never get a second chance to make a good first impression.

You make first impressions every day. They are the life-blood of business and professional people. You succeed or fail by the impressions you create in briefings, interviews, phone calls, sales meetings, conflict resolutions and the myriad encounters of everyday business life.

In the fast pace of a workday, deals can be won or lost, careers made or destroyed, relationships established or broken—all in a matter of minutes. In fact, in face-to-face encounters, you get only two to four minutes.[1] On the telephone you have just seconds.

First impressions are made of the things people notice about you during those crucial first minutes. They include your appearance, facial expressions, movement and tone of voice as well as your words—a rich lode of data with which to form a profile, a picture and an impression of you.

If that first impression is positive, it is like putting money in a bull market: your investment will pay big dividends. But a negative impression may be difficult, perhaps impossible, to change.

Power and credibility go to those who make good impressions, from a lawyer making opening arguments to a salesperson making a closing pitch, from an executive talking to the press to a politician talking to the voters, from a manager appraising an employee to an applicant interviewing for a job.

The pages that follow offer a step-by-step description of exactly what happens when you meet someone for the first time. This information is based upon solid research by experts in many fields and upon more than a decade of my experience as a communications consultant to business and industry, a professor of speech communication and a business owner with offices on both coasts.

This book can help you manage the impression you want to make and will show you how to "read" other people. It will help you find answers to the four key questions that define a successful communicator:

- What do I LOOK like?
- What do I SOUND like?
- What do I SAY?
- How well do I LISTEN?

By answering these questions, you will have a great deal of valuable information about how well or how ineffectively you communicate. In this book, we will go beyond mere answers to give you immediate help on how to change or fine-tune your body language, tone of voice, choice and arrangement of words and style of listening. This book has a flexible format. You can work your way through each chapter in sequence or you can skip around, zeroing in on specific subjects.

Knowing what kind of communicator you are is critical to success, for communication is what we people – especially businesspeople – do most:

- As much as eighty-five percent of your day may be spent in some form of communication – most of it speaking with and listening to others, according to a survey of businesspeople conducted at Arizona State University's College of Business Administration.[2]

- The typical working American gives about a dozen "speeches" a year – oral presentations to staff, clients, community groups, labor unions and professional associations.
- You spend two to four times as much time talking on the telephone as you do using any other technology, including computers and word-processors. If you are an executive, you spend about fourteen percent of your day on the phone.
- Communication skills rate second only to job knowledge as important factors in a businessperson's success, according to one study of five hundred executives.[3]

Although nearly every waking moment is spent listening or speaking to someone or something, the truth is most of us haven't the faintest notion of what we look like, how we sound, what we say or whether we are good listeners. And yet scientific research verifies that when meeting someone for the first time, how you say something and what you look like when you say it are much more important than the words you actually speak.

If people aren't quickly attracted to you or don't like what they see and hear in those first two to four minutes, chances are they won't pay attention to all those words you believe are demonstrating your knowledge and authority. They will find your client guilty, seek another doctor, buy another product, vote for your opponent or hire someone else.

During your first few minutes of interaction with others, their attention span is at its greatest and their powers of retention highest: their eyes and ears focus on you and tell their brains what they see and hear. That process of creating first impressions is intriguing but somewhat predictable. Depending on the other person's background and expectations, as well as the context of the interaction, here is what experts tell us typically happens when you meet someone for the first time.

First, people tend to focus on what they can *see*. In fact, there is a specific order by which others process information about you. While social scientists disagree on the precise sequence, that order generally appears to be:[4]

- color of skin
- gender
- age
- appearance
- facial expressions
- eye contact
- movement
- personal space
- touch

So much meaning is conveyed by these nine components of nonverbal communication that a number of communication experts believe "what you look like" constitutes more than half the total message. An astonishing fifty-five percent of the meaning is conveyed by facial expressions and body language alone.[5] And you haven't yet opened your mouth.

Next, people focus on what they can *hear*. When you speak, out comes a voice with additional characteristics, among them rate of speech, loudness, pitch, tone and articulation. These give the other person more information about you. Your voice – not including your actual words – may transmit as much as thirty-eight percent of the meaning in face-to-face conversations; it conveys a great deal more information on the telephone, because the other person is deprived of your body language—facial expressions, gestures, eye contact and all the rest.

Last, and certainly least in terms of those first few moments, the other person gets around to your words, which contribute a mere seven percent to the meaning.

It's not that your words are unimportant. But if others do not like what they see, or if they get past your body language only to be stopped by something in your voice, they may not care at all about what you say. Their minds already may be made up, their first impressions indelibly formed.

What Do I LOOK Like?

What happens in this process is akin to programming a computer: your audience takes in a number of "bits" of information about you, forming a composite, or pattern, of you. If not stopped by one variable, such as race or gender, it moves down the list to the next one, and so on—until all of you has been "read" and "processed."

If you walk into a meeting of people you don't know and you are the only one not wearing a suit, for example, you likely will stand out. As research by psychologist Nancy Henley points out, if you are the only man in a meeting of women, you will command attention because your gender has more initial power and authority.[6] (The opposite would likely not happen: one woman in a roomful of men might be ignored.) But if you are a black sales rep assigned to a territory of predominantly white clients, your skin color will be noticed, and negative stereotypes may affect the reception you are given.[7]

If your skin color, gender or appearance aren't "unexpected" or unusual, the perceiver then looks to your face, posture, gestures and the amount of personal space you occupy for further clues in forming an impression. All of this takes mere seconds, predictably in the sequence outlined earlier.

It might be useful at this point to recall the psychological notion of "figure and ground." Sometimes, what people notice about you stands out above everything else and becomes *figure* (such as race, gender and perhaps appearance); at other times, these very characteristics blend in and become *ground*. Thus, depending on the background and experience of the perceiver, significance may be given to a "part" of you that has little to do with your skills or expertise – your handshake, for example, or how quickly you speak – rather than to your qualifications or your verbal message.

With so much of the meaning garnered from body language alone, the question, "What do I LOOK like?" takes on special significance, as Chapter Two points out. While the weak grip in your handshake, the accent in your voice, or the frown on your face may have nothing whatever to do with the "real" you or the purpose of the interaction, the other person may never get beyond those characteristics to what you are saying.

What Do I SOUND Like?

Having processed the nonverbal information about you, the person seeing you for the first time now turns to the next source of information: your voice. Here again, as psychologists, speech therapists and others confirm, a great deal of information becomes available. Your voice tells a lot about your personality, attitude and anxiety level – it is a touchstone against which to relate and compare your words.

Experts in productivity and worker morale, for example, have uncovered fascinating evidence that supervisors' voices can affect employee performance. The intriguing work by industrial psychologist Sandra Seagal shows that the communication effectiveness and management style of executives can be determined – with a high degree of reliability – by studying their vocal attributes.[8] In her system, which has some empirical verification, focus is on auditory cues, especially pitch levels and rates of speech. By listening to vocal cues, Seagal can, with surprising accuracy, describe a person's "mental focus, precision, collaborative skills, flexibility, endurance, risk-taking abilities and performance levels."[9] So, by monitoring their own voices and those of others, managers and executives can focus attention on making improvements.

Answering the question, "What do I SOUND like?" can have big payoffs in formal situations, such as job interviews, press conferences, oral presentations or questioning witnesses. It also helps in more powerful ways: you can learn to recognize signs of tension and stress in your own voice and in the voices of others, as well as to use one of several vocal characteristics – such as rate or loudness – to energize an audience, client or jury.

Chapter Three examines this remarkable and irreplaceable instrument, discussing each vocal variable and how you can make changes and refinements. It suggests how to keep your voice strong and healthy and recommends techniques for monitoring your voice as you talk. Among other things, the information you'll learn should dispel old myths about deep, loud, low-pitched voices being the only way to sound powerful. Through analysis of your own voice, you will learn which aspects you want to work on and which ones you should leave alone.

The advisers to one recent candidate for the U.S. Senate did exactly that, because their client had a high-pitched voice accompanied by a slight lisp. Despite work with a voice coach, he made little progress. But he passed visual inspection easily and did well in small-group interactions. So, his advisers kept him as quiet as possible for as long as they could. They used a narrator with a deep voice for the candidate's campaign commercials, relied extensively on print for ads and avoided debates, press conferences and broadcast interviews. He won handily.

What Do I SAY?

If nonverbal and vocal communication constitute more than ninety percent of the message during the first few moments, why bother with language at all? Because you want to enhance and exploit that initial positive impression to communicate effectively the matter at hand. To do this, you must know what to say.

That's why verbal skills, as you will see in Chapter Four, must be suited to audience, situation and topic, and must support and balance the nonverbal and vocal messages already conveyed.

Let's take a brief look at a communicator who has put it all together – body language, voice and words. He's Arthur Bergman, fictional chief executive officer of Consolidated Brands.

Consolidated Brands' image was built around its personal relationship with customers. Arthur Bergman personally made it a point to further that image. Even so, the angry consumers gathered in a knot outside his door were surprised when his secretary ushered them into his office.

Bergman stood up, came around his desk and shook hands with each, asking names and giving his as he moved among them. He motioned for them to sit and, as they began taking their places, he perched on the edge of his desk.

He waited patiently, looking directly at each person; one hand rested on his desk, the other on his leg. Finally, Bergman opened his suit jacket and began speaking in a friendly but strong voice: "I understand you have some concerns about one of our new products. I'd like to hear them."

Bergman's style is a good example of a balance between what is said and how it is said. On a higher level it also mirrors the style of his company: open, reasonable and accessible—but in control and powerful. From the hospitality of his secretary to his skills in using the trappings of his position, Bergman created an atmosphere of openness and calm. He disarmed the angry consumers by recognizing the legitimacy of their concerns and listening to them.

Yet Bergman admitted nothing. Nor did he allow the group to control the confrontation. His every movement commanded respect, from his seemingly casual position overlooking them to his direct eye contact, from his strong but warm voice to his clear, straightforward language. Even his choice of words conveyed a recognition of the issue without defending his company or discussing solutions. Productive discussions can come later on.

The Importance of Consistency

Bergman provides testimony to the need for all three channels of information—body, voice and words—to work together to support one another: *what* he said was reflected by *how* he said it.

This matter of balance between language and delivery is critical in making positive first impressions. When one channel is "out of sync" with another, a double message may be communicated. The other person is left to figure out which to believe—what you said or how you said it. Studies show that most people tend to believe your body language and your tone of voice over what you say.[10] Your actions truly do speak louder than your words. People believe what they can measure, and that is what their eyes and ears tell them.

Let me illustrate the importance of consistency by telling of a client referred to me by his company. This fast-track executive feared his career was being derailed by those he knew didn't like or trust him. He confessed to not knowing why they felt that way because, as he put it, "I get results."

During the first few minutes in my office, he invaded my personal and professional space by dragging his chair up to my desk and patting me on the shoulder, calling me by the first name on my business card (although only my Mom uses it) and frequently interrupting me.

He *spoke,* however, of "teamwork," of sensitivity to his employees' feelings and of the need for ongoing, two-way communication with his staff.

The disparity between what he said and the way he acted was so great that I questioned his desire to change his behavior. Given his tendency to dominate in the presence of a stranger – and an assertive one at that – one could imagine his domineering behavior among fellow workers.

This executive's insensitivity, clearly manifested in his poor listening skills and intimidating body language, could spell the end of his rise to the top, unless he is willing to change. A study by the Center for Creative Leadership, a nonprofit research and educational institution, found that "insensitivity to others was cited as a cause for derailment more than any other flaw" in the men (no women were studied) who fell short of ultimate success.

There may be times, of course, when you want to risk a discrepancy between what you say and how you say it – when summarizing an opposing client's actions before a jury, for example, when concealing your position in delicate negotiations, or perhaps when you are furious at your boss. The point is to *know* when your communication channels are inappropriate and inconsistent and to understand the problems such dissonance may create.

Let me say it again, for it cannot be overstressed: in interpersonal communication, there must be an ongoing and perceived consistency between what you say and how you say it. Trust and, ultimately, success are built upon such consistency.

Understanding the nature of consistent communication can be a powerful tool. You can intensify something you wish to communicate, for example, by giving the same message in two or more channels. Telling new employees how glad you are to have them aboard will help build an even greater level of trust if you smile while you say those words and speak with sincerity and warmth. Being visible and accessible to your staff and customers gives power and meaning to statements about "open communications" and "participatory management."

Such power can extend beyond your own ability to communicate. By understanding how appearance, voice, words and other verbal and nonverbal characteristics reflect personality, attitude and feelings, you gain a valuable tool for "reading" other people – friends and foes alike. You gain powerful advantage over those with whom you do business.

In addition to the interpersonal benefits from consistent, positive first impressions, there are important economic considerations. Think about this next time you overhear an employee being curt to a disgruntled customer or a supervisor chewing out a colleague in front of a client: it costs five times more to create a new customer than to keep an existing one, according to a 1983 study by the Direct Selling Foundation. Moreover, an unhappy customer will tell nearly a dozen others about a bad experience and thirteen percent of *them* will tell twenty others. And on and on.

How Well Do I LISTEN?

Some top executives in a large New York bank neglected to consider the impact of first impressions when they decided tellers would wait only on customers with five thousand dollars or more in their accounts. Others were relegated to automated teller machines. Perhaps one reason so many customers rebelled and took their business elsewhere was that machines can't listen. This bank happened to be one with a solid reputation for listening, so it quickly rescinded that policy.

Listening is the final component in making positive first impressions—it is the other half of the communication process.

How many of us forget it takes two to communicate? Recall your own experiences where others have been such poor listeners you've not bought their products, not hired them, not believed them or simply not wanted to talk to them. We may look good, sound fine and even say the right things, but still blow it by not listening, or by listening in an inappropriate manner.

Chapter Five helps you answer the question, "How well do I LISTEN?" Consider the importance of the listening process: the higher you go in your profession, the more of your working day is spent listening to others. Moreover, some styles of listening are more appropriate to certain kinds of messages than others.

Listening is a skill that can be learned and practiced. And, as you'll see, it can make you a more powerful communicator.

Putting It All Together

By now you may be asking yourself, "How can I be my natural self if I have to worry about what I look like and how fast I talk when it's all I can do to put together two consecutive intelligent sentences under the pressure of meeting somebody for the first time?" You're right. Such moments are too important to be worrying about body language or tone of voice, or even choice of words. But just like the briefing papers you review before an important meeting, these matters of communication should be studied before the interview, before the performance appraisal, before the make-or-break presentation. Without such preparation, all of the salient facts and key selling points you have memorized may be for naught.

That is why you might want to take each communication channel in sequence, choosing which new behaviors you want to practice along the way to help make them part of your automatic response system. Chapter Six can help you pull it all together. It offers a guide to resources, people and training programs available to help you solve specific problems, even if you're on a limited budget.

Perhaps you are saying to yourself what a participant in one of my workshops once said, hands on hips, brow furrowed and voice stern: "I don't believe that my words are so unimportant; people just have to listen to what I say and take me for what I am." And I did—I took him to be an angry, threatened individual and moved on to another person's question, asked in a manner I took to be far less hostile.

There is a saying that "You cannot *not* communicate." Everything you do or say, don't do or don't say communicates something. The following pages offer information and advice on how to change things about you that you can (and want) to change. You will learn how to understand and accommodate those things you can't change. My goal is to help you communicate more effectively and to understand better those who communicate with you. As Robert Louis Stevenson once wrote, "To be what we are, and to be what we are capable of becoming, is the only end in life."

Chapter Two
What Do I LOOK Like?

Chapter Two

What Do I LOOK Like?

*H*ave you ever found yourself walking down a corridor en route, say, to a session at a convention in a large hotel, when you see a figure approaching? "Hmmm, that person looks familiar," you say to yourself. Drawing nearer, you realize you are approaching a large mirror, and the image it is reflecting is your own.

Most people cannot recognize themselves when their own image is unexpectedly reflected back to them. They have trouble simply remembering what they look like.

It's little wonder, then, that so many people flunk the most important question in the test of first encounters. They can't answer, "What do I LOOK like?"

Your answers are critical if you are to have any control over the impression you create in those precious first few minutes, because what people see—not what they hear you say—is what initially occupies their attention. And whether or not you actually are speaking, you always are communicating—through your movements, gestures, facial expressions, dress, even age and physique.

Your body language and appearance account for an astonishing amount of information about you. As pioneering research (by people such as Albert Mehrabian, Ray Birdwhistell, J. Reusch and W. Kees) showed and the current research (by such experts as Mark Knapp, Paul Ekman and Nancy Henley) continues to demonstrate, nonverbal communication alone can account for more than half of the "message" you convey.[11] And while some experts debate exactly how much information your appearance communicates, and whether the total impact of a message is equal to the sum of its parts, they do agree that nonverbal communication is vital.

Consider these factors about how you look as you prepare for your next "cold call," job interview, meeting with a new client, opening statement before a jury or daily encounter with unhappy customers:

- Nonverbal communication is the first and greatest source of impressions in direct, face-to-face interactions.
- It is the yardstick against which your words and actions are measured.
- It precedes and structures all subsequent communication.
- It tends to be even more heavily relied upon if your words give a contradictory message.
- It is one of the most revealing differences between powerful people and those with little or no power.

The range of situations in which first impressions are enhanced or hindered by appearance and body language is enormous. Here are just a few examples:

- Some IRS specialists suggest preparing for a tax audit by starting with what you will wear. The advice is sound. Dress the way you would for your business, be it a suit, blue jeans or dress. Go easy on the accessories (jewelry, expensive watches, hand-made leather briefcases). In short, don't flaunt your wealth, but don't upset the impression the auditor probably has of you from reading your tax returns.

- Personnel departments remind prospective employees that not only do interviewers tend to decide whether or not to hire primarily on personal impressions and not on résumés or credentials, but that they make up their minds within about five minutes of meeting you.
- Teachers with a positive view of humanity tend to use nonverbal cues that encourage student involvement – they smile and nod, listen actively and encourage physical closeness. Teachers with the opposite view tend to use nonverbal cues that discourage involvement – they smile less, occupy greater personal space and avoid direct eye contact.
- Employees are more productive when supervisors look at them, smile at them and touch them appropriately.
- Physically attractive defendants receive less severe recommended punishments from juries.[12]

Nonverbal communication – from appearance to facial expressions to movement – is the primary ingredient in the recipe people use to judge what's "attractive" in others. That is valuable information because physically attractive people have tremendous advantages in business and personal interactions. Studies show they are perceived to be more intelligent, more likable, more interesting and more credible than their less-attractive counterparts.[13]

The nonverbal factors focused on in this chapter can be changed – some to a greater extent than others, of course. The goal of these pages is to aid you in your personal inventory and assessment by reviewing specific nonverbal attributes in the order experts believe your body language is "read" or perceived.

At the end of this chapter is a summary of tips and a checklist to help you conduct your own "inventory" of nonverbal communication.

By the way, people sensitive to nonverbal cues tend to

be better adjusted, less dogmatic, more extroverted, more popular, more effective in interpersonal relationships and more accurate listeners. So, a valuable fringe benefit of understanding your own body language is that you will be able to read nonverbal cues of others in a new light.

Take a Good Look

Before beginning an inventory of your own body language, you might find it useful to refer to some samples. Take a look, for example, at any film clip or videotape of yourself. These are best because you can see yourself moving, gesturing, nodding or whatever. If you can get your hands on some video equipment, tape a few minutes of yourself as you sit, stand, walk – either alone or with others.

If that's not possible, photographs are next best, especially those that show you in action, not just staring into the camera. Study candid shots taken when you were talking to friends, playing with children, giving a presentation or working with colleagues.

As a last resort, get a full-length, lightweight mirror and prop it at one end of the room, where you can see your entire body.

It's important to have a tangible, accurate image from which to work rather than relying only on your mind's eye of what you look like. The best kind of "seeing" goes far beyond cursory glances into a mirror to make sure your tie is straight, your hair is combed, your beard is trimmed or your makeup is on correctly.

Although the focus of this chapter is how nonverbal communication cues influence the impressions others have of you, keep in mind that their perceptions will be filtered through one or more of these variables:

Expectations. Given one's cultural background, personality type, gender and status, certain things can be anticipated. A starch-collared female executive looking for an assistant might be unpleasantly surprised if the candidate who showed up was shy, casually dressed and stared meekly at the floor.

Context. Time, place, furniture arrangement, noise levels, interruptions, formality – all can affect the interactions. By influencing your surroundings, you can affect the communication process.

Communication display. You can choose how to display your gender, status and even your sense of self by the clothes you wear, how you move, what your face says and by other means. Consider your nonverbal attributes as neon signs and decide which images, if any, you want to advertise during an encounter. If you want others to focus on your gender, for example, you can do so by what you wear; if you want to convey confidence, focus on your movements.

That is why you should prepare yourself – verbally and nonverbally – for each new interaction with as much information as possible about the other person(s), the situation and the context.

From time to time, one component may have more importance than others, but each ultimately contributes to the complete picture of you that emerges. Clearly, some aspects of nonverbal communication are more easily *changed* (appearance and facial expressions, for example). Others are more readily *controlled* (the face, as opposed to gestures). And some nonverbal attributes are *beyond our control* (including gender and skin color), but may figure so strongly in initial interactions that people may not get beyond them to hear the words you speak.

Given the order in which your nonverbal elements are read or noticed by those forming first impressions, let's look at the roles of skin color, gender and age.

Color Barriers

Despite attempts to overcome prejudices, skin color remains the most dominant characteristic of physical appearance in this society. Depending on the attitude of the other person and the context of the interaction, skin color will stand out if it doesn't meet expectations – a black salesperson assigned a territory of suburban department stores, for example.[14]

Each will be observed and may, in fact, stand out by virtue of skin color alone. But if others are the same color as you, that fact will likely go unnoticed and they will zero in on the next physical attribute.

In situations where you think your skin color may be a negative factor, at least initially, you should seek to counter stereotypes by paying extra attention to your appearance, facial expressions, eye contact and other physical attributes.

A Matter of Gender

Gender also fosters stereotypes and positive or negative connotations. Just as being white carries more authority than being nonwhite, being male still means more power and authority than being female. This is particularly applicable during first encounters, in which men generally are given higher credibility by both men and women – even if the women have better credentials. This fact has been documented in many studies of meetings, conversations, television panel discussions and small-group interactions by communication scholars and sociologists.[15]

That's why other aspects of nonverbal communication are so important. They can help compensate or can move the viewer past race and gender and on to other attributes or information. Here's how a client of mine did just that:

Caroline Leed was hoping to be named the first female senior vice president in the history of her publishing company. At her final interview with the president, she wore her "power suit," but with a flower in the lapel. She strode into his office exactly on time with right hand extended, a warm smile on her face. She gave him a firm handshake and looked him right in the eye. She got the job.

Leed not only met expectations in terms of appearance, but also signaled her savvy and authority nonverbally: promptness, strong handshake, direct eye contact. And she used the smile, perhaps to counter any "unseemly" aggressiveness.

In a different vein, a group of female loan officers at an international organization called me to help them polish their negotiating skills. A role-playing situation I put them through made it clear they were "giving away the store" by their facial expressions. Not only did we work with mirrors to help them both see and feel what their faces were expressing, but I suggested they watch how their male counterparts often wore an interested-but-neutral countenance during difficult moments.

One advantage women have is that they tend to be more accurate than men in their reading of body language. But women may give up this edge with their own body language, for they tend to be more open in expressing attitudes and feelings. Their openness, therefore, can make them easier to read than their male counterparts. By virtue of training or socialization, men are proficient in concealing attitudes. They mask deception and inconsistency with neutral body language better than women do.

Each gender can learn from the strength of the other.

Women can become aware of how much information their body language may be transmitting and men can improve their interpersonal relationships by learning how to read others and express themselves nonverbally when the situation demands.

The Best Years of Your Life

Unlike skin color or gender, age is not itself a positive or negative variable, but takes on importance in direct proportion to your audience and its expectations.[16] For example:

- Sometimes being *young* is a disadvantage: if your patients expect an older physician, if your union assigns jobs by seniority or if your prospective employer is looking for someone with "experience."
- Sometimes it's a disadvantage to be *middle-aged:* if your CEO wants a more youthful vice president, if your company wants a younger-looking sales force or if your customers seem to gravitate to the older or younger clerks.
- It can be very tough to be an *older* person in initial interactions: if your résumé is put aside because you're "overqualified," if younger colleagues leave you out of social events or if your new boss wants "more dynamic" people to sell the new product line.

Although it may seem that you never are the right age at the right time, age is one of those nonverbal elements you *can* camouflage or highlight – in your appearance as well as with less obvious things, such as gestures and movement.

Say you want to downplay your age because you think you may look "too old."Among the advice given by image specialists (more about them in Chapter Six) is to select clothing that is stylish but not too trendy, perhaps with a flash of color in the accessories, and to have a modern hairstyle and not shrink at either coloring it or "supplementing" it with a hairpiece. Consider also cosmetic surgery (eye tucks, face lifts and nose jobs). Finally, move and gesture with energy and vitality.

To camouflage your age because you may look "too young," you might dress more conservatively—both in style and color—than others your age. Avoid long hair; shorter cuts can add five or ten years to your face. Carry quality accessories: a leather briefcase, real gold jewelry, a good-looking pen. Use makeup carefully so it doesn't draw attention to your face.

So, in a very few moments, other people have taken into account your race, gender and age, they have "registered" their impressions (positive, negative or uncertain) and they now may be ready to move on to other things about you they can see.

Most visible to them are your *appearance* and *face*. Image consultants zero in on these two elements of nonverbal communication because both are capable of much change and refinement and offer the communicator a wide range of choices. Let's consider each.

For Appearance's Sake

Appearance, a critical component of first impressions, includes much more than dress or clothing. It also takes into account:

- body type (size, weight, height);
- posture (sitting and standing);
- hair (or lack thereof);
- accessories (those you wear—purses, shoes, rings, bracelets, tie clasps, glasses; and those you carry—

pipes, cigarettes, briefcases, pens, notebooks and so on);
- smells (perfumes, body odors); and
- color (clothing, makeup).

It's not that people don't pay attention to appearance – Americans spend millions each year just on makeup, perfumes and cologne – it's that they pay so little attention to the *effect* appearance has on others and, in turn, on themselves.

I was at a conference with a client who gave a lecture at a podium in his three-piece dark suit. He looked elegant – until he started to move. Then the discomfort and stiffness showed. He moved and gestured awkwardly. His clothing seemed too new and unfamiliar for him. As soon as I could, I took him aside and suggested he take off the vest and, if possible, get into a pair of his favorite shoes. He looked relieved and after lunch returned to the seminar – sans vest, with loafers – confidence and relaxation evident in his face and movement.

Appearance can be the key to other people's assessments of you: your age, gender, socioeconomic status, group identification, likableness, power and authority.

I'm sure you've read about experiments in which well-dressed people who ask to borrow cab fare from strangers receive it and shabbier ones are ignored. Appearance has a direct impact on your credibility because so much information is conveyed. If skin color, gender or age don't stand out, appearance may become primary. Appearance influences other people's perceptions and may determine their attitudes. That's why people are more likely to respond to orders from someone in a uniform than from someone in civilian clothes (and a business suit – as opposed to jeans, open-collared shirt or sun-dress – *is* a uniform). That's also why people whose appearance suggests high status are treated measurably better than people whose appearance suggests low status. It's no wonder appearance can make or break a first impression, given all there is to look at and read into. In assessing your personal appearance and planning for future interactions, ask yourself these questions:

What are others' expectations?
- Do they expect me to wear casual or informal clothing?
- Do they expect me to be in a "uniform," to be dressed in formal clothes?

What will create the image I want, given the viewer's expectations or preconceptions?
- Should my clothing be of a certain style, color or fabric?
- Should I have accessories – such as jewelry, scarf or hat – and what should they look like?
- What color, style or height should my shoes be to complete the effect?

Am I comfortable with the results of what I am wearing and carrying (my hairstyle, perfume/cologne, color scheme, style of dress and so on)?

Such factors may have been on the mind of the personnel manager who put up a full-length mirror in the room where job applicants waited and hung above it a sign reading, "Would *you* hire this person?"

Remember that anytime you violate expectations – a dress code in your occupation, a degree of formality at a public ceremony or event, whatever – you assume risks. And with those risks may come sanctions, not the least of which may be a negative first impression.

The importance of appearance in establishing a positive

image cannot be overstressed. Experiment with your appearance, especially clothing and accessories:

- Study photos, old and recent, and note which ones you look good in and why. Was it your clothes? Hairstyle? Accessories? Weight?
- Get out your clothes and shoes and examine them. Step back and study them for colors and style. Which need to be cleaned, pressed, shined or mended?
- Study your image in a full-length mirror. Note your posture, the tilt of your head, the nature of your walk.

Note how your appearance affects your communication behavior – and how others behave toward you. Do you feel more confident when wearing a certain color or style? Do people compliment you, treat you with more respect or seem drawn to you when you wear certain clothing or carry specific accessories? You may be pleasantly surprised at what a difference these simple aspects of your appearance can make.

If examining your wardrobe doesn't produce any reaction at all, perhaps you should seek the advice of an image specialist. (See Chapter Six.) Appearance is such a critical factor that hiring such consultants can be a valuable investment that pays big dividends in making good first impressions.

Face Your Face

After your overall appearance, your face is the most visible part of you. Facial expressions are the cue most people rely on in initial interactions; they are the "teleprompter" by which others read your mood and personality.

Some intriguing research by Paul Ekman, the foremost authority on facial expressions, suggests that just the act of flexing facial muscles into the characteristic expressions of joy, anger or other emotions can produce effects on the nervous system that normally go with these emotions.[17] Ekman believes this is because the mechanics of facial expressions are tied closely to the autonomic nervous system. In fact, his preliminary work finds that the body responds to expressions of sadness differently than it does to those of happiness. The underlying message is that it might help to "put on a happy face" if you're nervous or fearful, or to put on a scornful one if you want to demonstrate anger or power. According to Ekman, your body will follow your face's advice, making you happier, angrier or whatever.

Facial expressions are critical in our relations with others. They are one of the few universal channels for expressing basic emotions that are not culture-bound.

Throughout the world, at least six emotions – surprise, happiness, anger, fear, disgust and interest – are expressed in the same manner. What *differs* from culture to culture is what causes these expressions and the "rules" for displaying them.[18] In Western countries, for example, a funeral elicits facial expressions of sadness, while in some Eastern countries a funeral may be a more joyful event. Anger or hostility may be reflected with a smile on a Japanese businessman's face, but his American counterpart may register a frown or no expression at all.

So unless you know what *caused* the emotion – its stimulus – you can't accurately judge the emotions registered on someone's face. The moral: don't interpret a facial expression entirely from your point of view. The other person's smile may not indicate agreement; it may indicate the person likes you – but doesn't necessarily like what you're saying.

The face is more easily controlled than other parts of the body, however, which makes it an often-unreliable source of information about what's going on inside its owner's mind. Other visual and audio cues are more useful for interpreting attitude and emotional states. (If you think someone is deceiving you, for example, study other body language and listen to tone of voice. Don't trust the face, especially if there's a discrepancy between what you see and what you hear.)

What might *your* face say to someone you are meeting for the first time? That you are angry because of your perpetual frown? That you aren't interested because your face looks blank? That you're nervous and anxious because you have a tight little smile?

The facial expressions you wear have been influenced not only by your cultural background but also by your gender and status. Consider these findings by researchers:

- High-status people smile less than low-status people.
- Women smile more than men, often in direct contradiction to the message they are conveying.
- A woman's smile is interpreted differently from a man's.
- Men tend to smile during efforts to deceive.
- Women who smile a lot are perceived as less effective managers.
- In male-to-male conversations, a smile wards off interruptions; in male-to-female conversations, a smile by the woman invites interruptions and is seen as a sign of submission.

Nevertheless, because of its versatility, smiling is the most important facial expression for communicating. It is a chief component of attraction and attractiveness. For example:

- People who like each other smile as a sign of that warmth.
- People who smile are considered more attractive than

those who don't. Moreover, they have much higher credibility than those with no facial expressions.

But smiling may create a double bind for women (and some men, especially those from non-Anglo cultures) because it often is interpreted as submissiveness, nervousness or "wanting to please." The problem is compounded if words or voice give a conflicting message.

What is critical, therefore, for both women and men, is that facial expressions be congruent or consistent with the tone of voice and the words being spoken. The more you know about what your face is saying, the more consistent you can make all three communication channels. Thus, if the context and message call for a pleasant expression, by all means smile. If not, don't.

Research explains why your facial expressions should be congruent with verbal and vocal channels:

- When a *positive* or *negative* message is being conveyed, the face is the primary cue people rely on.
- But when a message is *mixed* (for example, your face says you like the other person but your words or tone of voice demonstrate dislike), your face will tend to be ignored and your tone of voice believed.

Altering facial expressions isn't difficult, as you already know. With such flexibility, your range of expression is extensive. You may want, for example, to "put on" an exaggerated facial expression on some occasion to show surprise or excitement, because it is the expected response. Sometimes you may need to tone down, or de-intensify, a facial response, perhaps when the context doesn't call for much nonverbal display – when you are angry at a superior, for example, or arguing with a spouse in a public place.

Still other times, you can mask what is happening inside you by putting on an entirely different expression, one more appropriate to the setting or expectations. (Say you're negotiating with a competitor who has just said the "magic words," and you don't want to let on.)

The role facial expressions play in first-impression building is so important that early researchers into nonverbal communication focused on the face to the near exclusion of other nonverbal cues. Later studies broadened this research to include all the components we are examining in this chapter. But the original premise is worth remembering: the face is very revealing.

The Eyes Have It

From the broader map of your face, viewers may next focus on your eyes. Eye contact in initial interactions sometimes is referred to as the "enchanted evening" effect: eye engagement between two people can have explosive results without a word being spoken. By our looks alone we can evaluate others, show feelings toward them, invite them, discourage them, even dominate them.

Equal-opportunity specialists, such as one I once worked with at an electronics plant in Arizona, observe that a large number of complaints they receive from women – some of which lead to official charges of sexual harrassment – are based on nonverbal behavior of their male supervisors. "Ogling," "staring" and "visually undressing" are frequent complaints, and each is a form of eye behavior with serious and negative results.

It should come as no surprise that power, gender and culture also are critical factors in the nonverbal component of eye contact. Think about the powerful people you know. In eye contact, they probably differ from their subordinates and less assertive counterparts. They often look directly at the other person while talking but may look away when listening or hearing. They probably use eye contact to regulate conversations, especially to discourage interruptions. And they invite or discourage intimacy by the length of their gaze.

Research literature suggests that dominant people do indeed utilize eye contact quite differently than submissive people. In this country, especially among white males, direct eye contact may be considered one sign of power and authority. But there also is a growing effort to relate to people in less dominant, more personal, ways. Eye contact is one important nonverbal cue to others that you are listening to them and that you respect them – as an employee, for example, or as a person from a different background.

To effectively use eye contact, you must take into account cultural differences to avoid offending or alienating others. Some Americans of Asian descent and some American Indians, for example, find direct eye contact to be unsettling, even threatening – a sign of disrespect or hostility. And for them to make direct eye contact with you may be difficult or discomforting.

Again, as with other aspects of nonverbal communication, the more you know about the background of others, the more accurately you can interpret their eye contact and the greater flexibility you have in adjusting yours.

In addition to these cultural differences, there appear to be gender-based differences in eye contact as well. Here are a few of them:

- Women engage in more direct eye contact than men, especially while men are talking.
- Women, however, tend to avert their eyes more frequently than men, primarily while talking.
- Men stare more at women than vice versa.
- In face-to-face discussions, however, men engage in less direct eye contact while listening to women than while listening to other men.

Why these differences? Direct eye contact may be such an important indicator of status and power that it becomes the province of powerful people – in this country, that tends to be the male domain. Staring is an especially aggressive form of dominant behavior. Thus, those in power reserve the right to control the interaction by looking directly at a subordinate person while speaking but looking away while listening.

That tendency to manifest power in ways that separate and alienate people, that classify and stereotype them, may be fading as the search for what makes people more productive gains impetus. As Thomas J. Peters and Robert H. Waterman Jr. illustrate in their book, *In Search of Excellence,* "Attention to employees (not work conditions *per se*) has the dominant impact on productivity." Certainly, one way to let employees, customers, clients, patients, children, colleagues, friends and spouses know you are listening is simply to look at them while they talk.

Some men may avoid direct eye contact to prevent being interpreted as aggressive or seductive. But if a woman watches a man as a way of obtaining cues to appropriate behavior or to search for visual information, she may form a negative impression of a (well-intentioned) man deliberately avoiding eye contact. The result of this mess is akin to two ships passing in the night. Unless both make a conscious effort to shine their lights so each can see, they will pass unobserved, unnoticed and unappreciated.

A rule of thumb for effective eye contact is to make it direct, but adjust it according to comfort level. In situations where you (be you woman, minority male or white male) are dealing with Anglo men, *direct* eye contact throughout the interaction usually is a safe course.

All the Right Moves

If you're like most people, you haven't much awareness

of what you look like from the neck down, including how you sit, stand, move or walk. The first time you watched yourself on film or video, you may have felt disconcerted. Most of the time we see ourselves as cardboard figures – frontal view only – standing stiffly or moving forward.

Movement is a critical aspect in the presentation of a confident, assured impression, because walk and posture are closely tied to emotional state. For the observant, a wealth of information is available merely in how someone moves. The individual's level of confidence, degree of anxiety and efforts to deceive are evident to those who know what to look for. This is why trained observers pay close attention to how people sit, gesture and stand, and what they do with their hands and feet.

Your movements are so closely connected to relaxation or tension in the rest of your body that stiffness in your knees as you stand or in your arms as you grip something (a podium, a pen, the insides of your pockets) is transmitted up the body to the vocal cords, where the tension is amplified through your voice. (More on that in Chapter Three.)

If you are interested in the emotional state of another person, ignore the face – as you know, it's too easily controlled – and observe from the neck down. This part of the body reveals much more information. Look for:

- jerky, disjointed movements as a sign the individual is in conflict;
- slumped posture and shuffling movements as signals of depression or alienation; and
- frenetic, rushed walk or gestures as indicators of stress and anxiousness.

Compare these movements with the energetic, purposeful movement and carriage of people who are sure of themselves.

They *look* strong; moreover, they probably feel such confidence. They may even be "less muggable," as some New York City pedestrians were rated in a study that questioned convicted assailants.[19]

Here are some typical movement problems I encounter in my clients, all of whom are busy professionals:

Poor posture. Since childhood, we've all heard, "Sit up straight and quit slumping." That's still good advice. Good posture not only makes you look taller and more in command, but also is essential for proper voice control. But avoid sitting or standing in ramrod, military fashion. Keep your torso erect, not rigid, your shoulders even and both feet on the ground (not planted, but weight evenly distributed). This position, when sitting or standing, gives you flexibility to move or lean forward (both signs of interest and listening) or to lean or move back (suggesting disagreement, annoyance, boredom or relaxation).

Awkward gestures. People tend to forget they have hands until they are about to give a presentation – and then they don't know what to do with those things dangling from their sleeves. So hands are stuffed in pockets, underneath the table, behind a podium or around whatever is handy. Yet in nearly all cultures, other people want to see your hands; they wonder what's going on with them when they can't. It's best to hold your hands where they can be seen and where you can gesture naturally, to *illustrate* what you're saying or to *regulate* a conversation. (Try holding your hand up in a stop-sign gesture the next time someone tries to interrupt you.) When you do gesture, try to gesture toward your audience. Avoid wiping your nose, touching your face or scratching "private" parts of your body.

Inappropriate nodding. Nodding can serve important functions, so it must be used carefully. It can act as a "task function," for example, indicating agreement or encouraging further discussion. It can be a valuable sign you're listening. But it also can be a sign you are doing the "conversational work" to keep a dialogue going; that may be a sign of non-assertiveness. Nodding can be an unconscious habit signaling agreement to others when you don't mean that at all. Eliminate those nods that may convey an unintended meaning.

If you haven't thought about your walk, gait or pace, or how you move your head and arms, you may be missing some of the most interesting and revealing facts about yourself. By moving with confidence and energy and by striding with purpose, you are more likely to be perceived that way. Such movement also empowers you with more confidence.

A (Personal) Space Odyssey

Study a photograph of yourself with friends as you talk or relax. Note the distance between you and the others. It's probably a matter of inches, with one or more participants leaning in toward the others, perhaps touching someone, their faces tilted toward the person speaking. Compare that with the amount of space you maintained when a repair person came, when you met a new colleague, when you greeted a former client or patient. Then recall instances when your new boss stood over you while you sat at your desk, or the time you testified in court and the attorney for the other side put her hands on the railing of the witness box and leaned into your face.

In each case, your "bubble of privacy" depended on:

- your size, height and weight;
- your cultural background;
- whom you were with and how well you liked each other;
- how much power and authority was being wielded and by whom; and
- whether you were male or female.

Extensive research on the human being's need for a certain amount of space leads to the conclusion that we vary our needs slightly with the variables I've just mentioned, plus some others.[20]

How you guard your personal space and how big it is at any one instance is something you respond to unconsciously, often in reaction to someone else's movement. When you're attracted to someone you probably diminish your "shield." But when you approach the boss's desk, you probably remain seven to twelve feet away, unless encouraged to draw closer. When you fear others or are repulsed by them, you automatically extend your personal space. In brief, you expand or contract your personal space according to how intimate you want that encounter to be.

Here are some examples of the effect power, gender and culture have on the size of one's territory as well as some ways people defend their space or invade someone else's:

- High-status people are given more space in nearly all cultures than low-status people.
- High-status people tend to "own," and are granted, more desirable spatial positions (the proverbial "corner office," for example).
- Aggressive people tend to take up, and are granted, more space than less dominant people.
- Men generally occupy more personal space than women.
- Women's space tends to be violated more often than men's.
- Extroverts take up more space than introverts.

These examples suggest an important message: not only do powerful people take up more space and freely invade the space of others, but less powerful people actually *yield* space to them. During initial interactions with someone who doesn't know you, you may give an impression of personal power if you simply occupy more space when you stand or sit *and* if you do not move out of the way or allow invasion of your space by people attempting to dominate you. Interestingly, the research suggests you probably won't change the size of your territory, especially when standing, if you dislike someone; you will try to indicate that response by other cues, such as the way your body is angled, your gestures and your facial expressions. That's probably because you're hoping to convey the message in more subtle ways first. A sense of personal territory also is at stake and you may want not to back away. But you will sit or stand *closer* to someone you feel positive about.

So much for *personal* space. There's also *professional* or *working* space. You should use room arrangements, lighting, furniture, noise control and other environmental elements to your advantage. Display your best image. If you're short, for example, get people to sit; if you want privacy, change locations or move chairs. If you want quiet, shut out noises and distractions; if you want air, open a window or step outside. Whenever appropriate, be assertive about the environment in which you meet and greet people.

Touching Experiences

Physical contact, regardless of cultural background, is important for healthy development. Infants who are not cuddled, touched or stroked often grow into problem children with severe emotional needs. Our elderly suffer from "skin hunger" because they often receive little body contact or touch. The older most of us grow, in fact, the less frequently we touch and are touched.

As with eye contact, touching behavior is fraught with misunderstanding. It is the only aspect of nonverbal communication that involves physical contact with another person. Touching can be a powerful means of expression:

- A firm handshake may signal acknowledgment or equality; a limp handshake may mean lack of interest or timidity.
- A pat on the head or face can signal liking, but easily can be construed as condescension or paternalism.
- A thrust with one pointed finger can indicate dislike or anger, while a soft touch with an open hand may reveal positive feelings.

One of the difficulties of touch, especially with people who don't know each other, is exactly what to construe from it: Intimacy? Status? Parity? Civility? Openness and warmth? The possibilities are endless.

Touch differs from culture to culture. Relative to other regions, North America has a noncontact culture. We may touch our pets more than we touch members of our families. Keep cultural differences in mind, therefore, when encountering someone who gets you in a bear hug or kisses you on both cheeks—or resists *your* touching by offering an outstretched hand.

One reason why we use tactile communication much less than other nonverbal behaviors may be the importance power, gender and status play:

- Low-status people (employees) are touched more than high-status people (employers).
- Children are touched more than adults.
- Women are touched more often and on more parts of their bodies than men.
- People touch those they like much more than those they dislike.

The person who initiates touch tends to have a higher status or a more dominant personality.

> A colleague, a young, new female professor, came to me furious because her department chairman always patted her on the rump. We worked out a verbal strategy whereby she would describe his behavior, tell him how it humiliated her and ask him not to touch her any more – classic steps in assertiveness. It worked for awhile, but then he slipped back into his old ways. One day she rushed in triumphant. "He'll never touch me again!" she declared. "He just patted my rear and asked how I was. I reached over and patted his genital area, and said, 'Just fine.' He turned scarlet and fled!"

While I don't advise such direct action, you sometimes can handle inappropriate touching behavior by returning it in kind – sort of holding up a mirror to the offender.

Because the consequences of touching often are risky and subject to a wide range of interpretations, consider a firm handshake the safest, least controversial and most equitable form of touch to use when meeting a stranger.

Putting It All Together

First impressions begin with what others see in you and you in them. It takes only two to four minutes to make that impression positive or negative. More than half of the meaning is carried in those nine nonverbal components – nine distinct cues, some controllable, others not very much, but all there for the picking by the observant viewer.

Here are three key points to remember:

1. The more you know about each of those nine components and the context in which they operate, the higher your chances for conveying the image you want.

2. The more you know about the culture, gender and status of others, the more accurately you can predict their expectations and the more you can tailor your nonverbal cues to meet those expectations.

3. The more consistent you can make what you say with how you say it, the more favorable that first impression will be.

It's too risky in those first few moments to try out double meanings, too soon to risk sarcasm. You can't expect your words to make up for a poker face, nervous smile, poor eye contact, tentative movements, timid handshake or pat on the fanny. The other person may not make the effort to resolve the paradox, return the look, figure out the sarcasm or ask for an explanation—he or she simply may turn you off and label you unfavorably.

Time is of the essence in new interactions, which makes it perfectly understandable that other people use whatever information they have available to help make their decision about you. Call it your packaging, your cover, your style—call it whatever you want, but never underestimate the power of nonverbal communication.

How To Make Your Body 'Say' What You Mean

1. Be consistent in all three channels – body, voice and words – unless you deliberately choose to throw people off balance. If so, consider the risks in such a strategy.

2. Dress for the job, client or account you have in mind, not neccessarily the one you presently have. You may need to dress more formally or informally for some clients to create the optimum working environment.

3. Spend money on a professional-looking wardrobe; if necessary, get a specialist to help you. Knowing you look good goes a long way in helping you feel good.

4. Know what your face says. It may be the most controllable nonverbal cue, but it also is the one people rely on to gauge your attitude, feelings and emotional state. You might be able to "fool" yourself into feeling better than you really do simply by smiling.

5. Smiling and head nodding are the most powerful non-verbal cues in social attraction.

6. A blank expression ranks lowest in terms of attractiveness, power and credibility.

7. Start with direct eye contact as your point of reference, and adjust from there. It's a more powerful cue than averting your eyes.

8. If you're awkward about making eye contact, look at the person's forehead or hairline. Unless the other person is standing very close to you, it is difficult to tell whether you're avoiding direct eye contact.

9. Walk briskly (not too fast or too slowly), stand and sit "tall," and you will look and feel more confident. Your voice will repay you by sounding strong and resonant.

10. Gesture with purpose and always toward your viewer. Don't make cramped gestures or "fly-flicking" movements. Don't fiddle with coins, bracelets, keys, pens, ties or other objects.

11. Establish a "bubble of privacy" and deal assertively with those who violate it.

12. Touch appropriately and deal assertively with those who touch you inappropriately. For both genders a firm handshake is best in most professional settings.

13. Occasionally monitor your nonverbal cues. Look carefully at yourself in a mirror; use photographs, film or videotape to examine your body language. As you begin to make changes, get new samples of what you look like.

14. If you have doubts, get help from a close friend, spouse, sympathetic colleague or helpful boss. Consider hiring an expert (see Chapter Six for guidelines).

Chapter Three
What Do I SOUND Like?

Chapter Three

What Do I SOUND Like?

*T*he pen may be mightier than the sword, but neither is mightier than the mouth, especially when it comes to creating first impressions. Consider that attractive new person you saw recently and how disappointed you were upon hearing a shrill, strident voice grating on your ears like chalk on a blackboard. Or recall the time you ventured into a computer store only to leave quickly at the rush of high-tech terminology coming at you rapid-fire from the salesperson.

Recall, on the other hand, the calm, reassuring voice at the other end of the telephone line when you called the police to report a burglary, or the energetic, confident tone of the consultants you hired as they reviewed for you their new development plan.

Voice communication is second only to body language as a means of communication in initial interactions – as much as thirty-eight percent of the meaning is communicated by voice qualities (but not words), according to those whose research has focused on this area. In a telephone conversation, the voice is, of course, the most important channel.

Talking probably occupies a large percentage of your day. The higher you go in your career, the more time you will spend speaking (and listening – more on that in Chapter Five). Yet we take our speech for granted. We abuse our vocal mechanism with cigarettes, alcohol, caffeine and poor nutrition. We weaken it with stress and exhaustion. We tire it and strain it by talking loudly with improper support and insufficient breath supply. In short, we forget that a voice is irreplaceable, so unique in its "print" there's not another one like it on Earth.

"What do I SOUND like?" is a question to ask often. How you shape and control the sound waves you produce determines whether your voice sounds raspy or pleasant, soft or loud, mushy or clear, rapid or slow, high-pitched or low — effective or counterproductive.

The Voice of Authority

In face-to-face interactions, it isn't enough to be physically attractive. The moment you open your mouth you either confirm or deny an initial impression. (Certainly you've heard the sage wisdom that it's better to keep your mouth shut and let others assume you're an idiot than to open your mouth and remove all doubts.) If you sound harsh and abrasive, you probably will be viewed as harsh and abrasive. If you sound timid and insecure, you probably will be considered as such. And if you sound strong and confident, chances are you will be thought of that way.

Speech plays a vital role in making first impressions. Your listeners don't know if their initial impressions are valid; they have only limited information – your body language and appearance – before them. That pool of information grows considerably, however, when you begin to speak. They may *see* an attractive person – friendly face, well groomed, confident in movement and all the rest – but what do they hear when you open your mouth? A nasal drone? A mushy slurring of words? A breathy voice that trails off? Or do they hear warm, pleasant tones? A voice with energy and variety?

It's important to understand that you hear your voice in a different way than others. You hear your voice as it echoes through your head; others hear your voice as it is transmitted directly through their ears. Thus the only way you can accurately answer the question, "What do I SOUND like?" is by listening to a tape recording of your voice.

The more you understand about your voice and how to control it, the more powerful it can be. The human voice, for example, affects the listener physiologically, which is one reason we are sensitive to nuances of sound:

- Speak *rapidly,* and your listener's heartbeat and adrenalin flow may increase and breathing may become shallow.
- *Shout* at someone and that person's blood pressure may rise.
- Speak *calmly,* slowly and quietly, and corresponding physical responses result.[21]

Your voice is a remarkable tool for reducing tension and anxiety, conveying calm and control or – should you find it necessary – for energizing situations, exacerbating tensions and stimulating activity. Not only does your voice affect others, it is a finely tuned barometer of your own physical and emotional states:

- It can reveal your stress levels long before other physical signs of stress.
- It reflects your level of fatigue.
- It indicates your emotional state.

Unless you become sensitive to the characteristics of your own voice, you won't be able to make necessary changes that can reduce your stress and help relieve your fatigue.

By understanding the nature of the human voice, you gain advantages throughout your personal and business life. Take, for example, a situation where you are expected to make rather sudden decisions about your employees' readiness to take on an important new project. If you listen carefully to their voices–pitch levels that go higher and higher, quickening rates of speech, increases in loudness–you may discover you have an exhausted staff that would benefit from a few hours off, a change of pace or even a change of environment.

Tune into voices and you will be more attuned to others' feelings, which aren't easily masked vocally. And, most important, you can regulate your own voice to make the impression you want–a powerful tool in the business world.

How to achieve such powers? It requires increasing your knowledge of vocal sounds. In this chapter, you will use your own voice as the model for analysis and improvement.

To begin, tape-record three samples of your voice, two to three minutes each, at different times:

- first thing in the morning, when your voice is relaxed and fresh;
- early afternoon, when stress and exhaustion tend to be high; and
- late evening, when you're relaxed but tired.

These samples could include conversation with others–perhaps something you've dictated to a secretary or said on the phone–and some reading aloud of an editorial, favorite story or poem.

You can use the samples: to understand the importance of good breathing; to learn the vocal characteristics of rate, loudness, pitch, quality and articulation; and as the basis for exercises aimed at improving each of these. You may want to get feedback from others, including friends, colleagues and professionals, such as speech therapists or voice coaches. And you may want to compare your voice to good vocal role models.

With this information you then can proceed to draw up a plan of action for improving various aspects of your voice, using the exercises at the end of this chapter.

Don't worry if you've never taken a speech course, acted in a play, gone to Toastmasters or sung in a choir. You *have* read aloud, talked at meetings, given briefings and negotiated on the phone. You probably spend more than a third of nearly every workday speaking, which means you've had lots of practice. Every voice can be changed if its "owner" is committed to working on it, but the key to improvement is hearing how your voice sounds to others and then implementing ways to vary one or more of its attributes.

A Breath of Fresh Air

Good speech begins with an ample supply of oxygen. Right now, take in a breath of air; now, let it out s-l-o-w-l-y and smoothly. You've just added fresh oxygen to your bloodstream and replaced carbon dioxide waste. The oxygen provides vital nutrients to your brain (and helps reduce stage fright). Moreover, your lungs now are filled with an oxygen reservoir from which the air stream for creating "voice" is derived.

By the way, you don't need a lot of air to speak well; it's what you do with what you have that's important. One key factor, though, is *how* you breathe. During plain old garden-variety breathing – in and out, in and out, without talking – the ratio of inhalation time to exhalation time is about one-to-one (for every second you spend inhaling, you spend one second exhaling). When you breathe for speech, however, that ratio jumps to one-to-seven. That means you take in breath quickly but sustain the exhalation longer.

How deeply you breathe bears no relationship to how loudly you talk, so you can forget that old adage about filling the "tanks" up to the top – abdomen to shoulders, tightening in a soldier-like fashion all the way – and then blasting your words out with all you've got. What is critical for good voice production is to relax as you breathe, drawing in air deeply – preferably from your diaphragm – and releasing it efficiently.

Why breathe from the diaphragm and not from the chest area? Several reasons:

- By breathing from the abdomen you have two sources or cavities of air – your stomach and your chest – instead of one.
- "Diaphragmatic" breathing takes pressure off your shoulder area. That reduces throat strain and neck tension, which cause inefficient and unpleasant voice production.
- The shape of the thoracic cavity (the area within your rib cage) means that high-chest breathing takes more energy. The diaphragm's cone shape (it is broader at the base than at the top) allows it to be raised and lowered easily to change volume.
- Problems of loudness, voice quality and the ability to vary rate of speech often can be corrected by shifting breathing from the chest to the diaphragm.

A bonus of breathing with your diaphragm is its role in reducing stress and tension by providing the body, especially the brain, with a greater, longer-lasting supply of oxygen.

Are you a high-chest breather? You can tell by watching yourself in a mirror as you talk. Do your shoulders go up and down as you breathe? Then you're a "high-chester" and a likely candidate for vocal stress and problems of voice control. You'll benefit, I guarantee, by regularly doing the breathing and relaxation exercises at the end of this chapter, especially when you are under tension. If you remember nothing else about breathing, remember this: breathe slowly and calmly.

Good breathing is so essential to achieving a strong and pleasant voice – and making a good first impression – it's worth it to learn to breathe automatically from your diaphragm.

Five Steps To a Good Voice

With an understanding of breathing as the foundation to speaking well, take out your tape recorder, put it about three feet away and let's begin analyzing the voice on the tape you made. Listen for those five characteristics of your voice: rate, loudness, pitch, quality and articulation. Read my descriptions of each, then check your voice sample for the problems I describe. Try out the suggestions on how to make improvements and practice specific exercises.

1. Vary the rate. Tape recorder on, listen first to the rate at which you speak. You might even figure out how fast you talk by counting the number of words per minute (you can do this easily by counting the number of words for fifteen seconds and multiplying by four). You're an average talker if it's between 130 and 160 words per minute, but understand that your speaking rate will change according to several conditions: the size of the room and the audience, the amount of noise present, the level of difficulty of the material you are talking about and the emotional content of the material.

As you listen to the taped sample, ask these questions about your voice:

- Does it zip along so rapidly you seem to be gasping for breath?
- Is it so slow and regular as to be too predictable, monotonous or dull?
- Are your words run together?
- Are there pauses for emphasis?
- Does the rate sound the same throughout?

How fast *should* you talk? It depends upon several factors:

- *Physical environment.* You might talk more slowly in a filled conference room than in a small room with just one other person.
- *Noise levels.* You might slow your rate down to compensate for the noise created by typewriters, phones or other people.
- *Nature of the material.* If you're emotionally involved in the topic (like your upcoming promotion or pet project), your rate probably will increase from the rate you use with "unemotional" topics (like small talk about the weather), unless you consciously control it.
- *Medium used.* A rapid rate is difficult to understand on the telephone because there are no nonverbal cues to help the listener understand (the same is true when speaking for radio broadcast).

A good rule of thumb is to vary your rate of speech, but to spend more time talking quickly than slowly. In fact, some new studies demolish the old stereotype of fast-talking people as slippery and shallow, and conclude that, in one-way communications (such as speeches and presentations), faster speakers are regarded as more intelligent, more convincing and more impressive, particularly if the speaker is male.[22] (The old stereotype that women who speak rapidly are nervous, anxious or flighty persists.) Fast talkers, by the way, average 160 to 200 words per minute, versus 110 to 130 for slow ones.

When you're meeting someone who has never heard you, start slowly if you're a fast talker and build to your normal rate. Remember, in those first few moments the other person has to digest all of that nonverbal information about you (how you look, dress, move and so on) before getting to your voice. My advice is that if you're a slow talker, especially when surrounded by rapid speakers, keep in mind the unfortunate tendency people have to stereotype you negatively. Try to pick up your pace in the opening moments.

One aspect of rate often overlooked and yet easiest to apply is that of the *pause*. Silence can help you stress points and build interest. One way audiences distinguish trained speakers from untrained ones, studies show, is the length and variety of pauses. By pausing you can gain and control attention – as long as your nonverbal actions correspond. The next time you are in conversation with a new acquaintance, pause as you talk but don't drop your eyes, look away or give other signals that you're finished; if you do, you can be sure you will be interrupted. The trick is to pause in a way that tells others you're . . . not . . . through . . . yet: keep your inflection up, hold your gestures aloft, maintain eye contact.

Fortunately, rate of speech can be refined more readily than any other vocal variable. In my experience as a speech professor, voice coach and theater director, I found rate the easiest vocal characteristic to vary. And when you control your rate of speech, you gain an advantage over your listeners, because people react physically to your rate. That's a valuable tool when you want to stimulate people or increase their attention span: simply pick up your pace. (Now you know why salespeople often talk at lightning speed.) Conversely, when you speak more slowly, drawing out vowels and putting in pauses, you can have a calming effect, lowering arousal levels and soothing stressed or anxious people.

It may be that by trying out just this one change in your voice you can lend your image an enthusiasm or dynamism it lacks. Particularly as we reach middle age, our voices lose flexibility and may take on a dull, lifeless quality. We may seem inhibited, our voices colorless, monotonous. These characteristics translate into voices that have little animation, whose pitch levels are constant, whose loudness or energy levels lack variety. It's as if a tendency to behave with more caution and conservatism has been translated into and even reflected by the voice. Such characteristics are not only disagreeable for those listening, but are fatiguing for you because you are only using one set of muscles.

Of all the attributes of voice discussed in this chapter, change of pace – variety in rate – is the greatest antidote to monotony.

2. Control the loudness. To answer that key question, "What do I SOUND like?" you must observe not only your rate of speech but also the vocal attribute of loudness or volume. All the knowledge you marshal won't help much if people can't hear you. Likewise, you can negotiate a contract over the phone holding a full hand of trump cards, but if you're talking so loudly that the other person has to hold the receiver two inches away, he or she may fold and call it quits. As you listen to your voice with as much dispassion as possible, recollect for a moment: do people ask you frequently to speak up? Do they often say "Huh?" or "What was that again?" Are you asked to repeat things? If so, those are cues your volume may be too low.

Or do people lean back or step away from you when you talk? They may be giving you nonverbal cues that you're talking too loudly. Have you had people on the other end of the telephone ask you not to shout? Or ask why you seem to sound agitated? Are you exhausted physically and emotionally at the end of a discussion? In each case, you probably are speaking with a vocal intensity inappropriate for the situation.

Consider meetings, conventions or rallies you have been to where speakers shouted into microphones because they forgot that the purpose of mikes is to amplify sound. Or recall your irritation when speakers talked in a volume so low they couldn't be heard beyond the front row.

The loudness levels you employ, whether in interpersonal conversation or before large groups, must take into account these factors:

- *distance* (how far you are from your listeners);
- *environmental noise* (from foot traffic to ringing telephones);
- *the situation* (an argument or an intimate dinner); and
- *the material* (a pep talk to employees or an individual perfomance appraisal).

Failure to adjust these may cause the listener to tune out and turn away.

As you work to control your loudness levels and make them more interesting and effective, keep in mind that the strength of your vocal signal must be related to noise levels:

- To compete on fairly equal terms with the noise in your environment, be loud enough to be heard.
- Manipulate the environment as much as possible to reduce noise and keep your signal in focus: shut doors; find quiet places; minimize interruptions; talk directly into the telephone or microphone, not to the side of it.

Another prerequisite for loudness is wanting to be heard. In making good first impressions this means looking *at* people, not down at the floor; opening your mouth to let the sound out rather than trapping it inside; and being alert to environmental interference so you can make immediate adjustments in your voice levels.

Be sure to speak distinctly, to open your mouth and let the sounds out. People hear better when they can see your lips move. (This is as true for people who hear well as it is for those with hearing impairments.) Men with beards or mustaches may need to do a little trimming of the hair on their upper lips or else take extra care in how they form their sounds.

Loudness is not the same as shouting; it is intensity and force. I once heard actor Sir John Gielgud say that loudness is a focusing of the sound to pierce the armor of the air mass and reach the intended listener. He had us move to the back of a theater while he stood upstage and *whispered* a soliloquy from *Hamlet*. We heard every single word.

Effective speakers use loudness differently from poorer speakers. Good speakers:

- change loudness levels more frequently than poorer speakers;
- use less vocal power on unimportant words, such as articles (*the, a, an*), conjunctions (*and, or, but*) and prepositions (*with, into, about*);
- have better breathing habits, marked by slow and steady movements of the diaphragm, rather than irregular, upward movements of the chest and diaphragm; and
- use inhaled air more efficiently.

Changes in vocal power allow you to stress key words (especially *action* words, such as verbs) or lower your volume almost to a whisper to emphasize other key words and phrases.

Loudness levels demonstrate your conviction, assist the listener in comprehending your points and show comparison and contrast. An executive from a public utility company I worked with responded to press queries about utility rate increases by dropping his volume to near-inaudibility as he mumbled his answer. Reporters branded him evasive and lacking in knowledge. By learning to vary his loudness, he projected a more confident and trustworthy image.

The best guideline for volume is to establish a basic level appropriate to audience size, environmental noises and the nature of the situation, and then adjust that level to lend interest and variety. In other words, turn the dial up or down as the material, competing noise and other factors dictate.

3. Fine-tune the pitch. Pitch is the highness or lowness of the sound. Dan Rather and Ronald Reagan have low-pitched voices. Jimmy Carter and Lee Iacocca have higher pitches. Bette Davis and Lauren Bacall have lower-pitched voices than Barbara Walters and Jane Fonda.

Knowing your own pitch can give you greater control over the impressions you make because listeners form all sorts of judgments about you—often with startling accuracy—based on your tone of voice. Your socioeconomic status, age, attitude and trustworthiness all can be detected in your pitch by a careful listener.[23]

Increased familiarity with your pitch levels can help you spot vocal inconsistencies that may contradict your own body language or words. Moreover, it can help monitor your stress levels. After an exhausting day, for example, you may hear your pitch become higher. It probably will rise during intense emotional displays, such as anger, fear or surprise.

With your tape recorder on, listen for these typical problems as you assess your tone of voice:

- *A rising or upward inflection at the ends of sentences.* You aren't likely to buy something from a salesperson who tags a questioning tone to the ends of declarative sentences, such as "This is a nice car?" or "I see you like our selection of furniture?" Make certain your own statements have proper inflection. In English that means your tone comes down at the end of most sentences to signal completion and certainty. Improper inflection gives the impression of tentativeness and powerlessness.

- *A singsong quality to the pitch.* Vary tones for the sake of meaning, not variety. Remember your kindergarten teacher's singsong instructions? That sort of voice in a businessperson gives an immediate impression of immaturity or passivity. The melody interferes with the message.
- *Monotony.* Avoid a lack of variety in pitch levels. That's the flip side of "singsong." You may hear that in a bored employee or an uninterested supervisor. They may interpret your own monotonous voice as a lack of caring.
- *The "rain-barrel" effect.* If you're producing sounds far back in your throat, the raspy, gargling voice that results may convey gruffness, impatience or hostility.

Before you start trying to solve problems you may hear in your tone of voice, keep in mind one important thing: do not try to change your basic pitch. Leave it alone. When people try to relocate their average pitch, serious vocal disturbances may result, including vocal strain. Ignore those old saws about going up and down the musical scale until you find your optimum pitch; that simply is not accurate.

Instead assume your physiological maturation has been as normal in your larynx as in any other part of your body. If you have normal vocal cords that vibrate under normal tension, then the frequency at which they most often vibrate is the best, the most effective and the most efficient frequency for you. That is your optimum pitch level, the one you can use to produce sounds with the least effort. Shifting by a marked degree from that habitual range can spell trouble.

What is *your* average tone or pitch level? It's the one you return to more than any other, as you will hear throughout your tape-recorded samples.

When you are under stress and anxious, you will notice your pitch probably becomes higher; that's because your vocal cords are tense. When they're tense, they get tighter; the tighter they get, the faster they vibrate. The resulting tone will be higher, just like strings on a guitar.

When you are relaxed, your pitch will be lower and more resonant. Again, the vocal cords are relaxed and reverberate less, producing a lower, more pleasant tone. And when you are sick, especially with a cold, the pitch may sound quite unlike your normal one, often because the vocal cords are coated with phlegm, distorting the tone.

All of these changes are perfectly normal. If monitored, they can be moderated by such simple techniques as:

- pausing to breathe in fresh oxygen;
- lowering the volume, which usually brings down the pitch; and
- doing some isometric exercises in the throat and chest area to break the tension.

The relaxation and breathing exercises at the end of this chapter can help you resolve pitch problems and make this vocal attribute more effective.

Good speakers have a wide range of pitch. Since most people have a range of at least one octave, it's a waste of time to try to extend your range – unless you're aiming for the opera. It would be more useful for you to shed your inhibitions and explore the range you already have.

Rate, loudness, pitch – any one of these vocal attributes may convey more about your feelings toward the subject or the listener in those first few moments than all your words combined. Pitch can be modified a lot, while rate and loudness are capable of much change and variation – if you understand the role each speech component can play in making an impression.

4. Monitor vocal quality. "He sounds like a foghorn." "Her voice is like listening to a record under water." "His voice is full of mush." These are descriptions of the vocal attribute of *quality,* also called "timbre." Your voice's quality distinguishes it from any other voice in the world. You want your voice to match the highest professional stature; you don't want a quality that connotes timidity, unreasonableness or immaturity.

It is valuable to be familiar with the five factors that make up voice quality:

- *Vocal structure* – it's determined by the size of your larynx and the length and width of your vocal cords.
- *Resonance chambers* – the sound bounces around in your throat, nasal cavities and mouth.
- *Breath supply* – the more efficient its use, the better the sound.
- *Stress* – your voice quality changes when you are relaxed or exhausted.
- *Fitness* – smoking, drugs, alcohol and caffeine can take their toll.

Millions of working Americans engage in what speech pathologists call "voice suicide" by striving to sound as authoritative, sexy or macho as possible. Many damage their voices, sometimes irreparably.

By knowing how your voice sounds under a variety of conditions, you will be able to avoid vocal abuse and maintain optimal voice quality.

To find out your own voice quality, listen again to your recorded sample. Be alert to six negative features that detract from tonal quality:

• *Nasality* – "talking through your nose" – a common and annoying problem.

Some nasality is important, but only for these sounds: *n, m* and *ng*. Remember Lily Tomlin's comic character, Ernestine, the telephone operator? Her voice irritates because of its nasality.

To find out if you're a nasal speaker, pinch your nose closed and say, "They ran fifteen miles, falling and stumbling near the finish." There should be vibrations in your nose only with the *n, m* and *ng* sounds. Now, hold your nose again and say aloud, "Woe, oh horse of mine." There should be no buzzing in your nose until the last word; except for "mine," the sound should come entirely from your mouth. If there are vibrations in your nose, you're probably a nasal speaker.

To correct nasality, simply open your mouth more to get those vowel sounds out. You may need to speak more loudly, articulate more actively and keep your tongue down and forward as much as possible. Nobody likes to listen to the whining, honking sounds of people who talk through their noses or through clenched teeth.

• *Breathiness* is what I call the "little-person syndrome." Women often suffer from this problem; they were socialized at an early age to speak in a breathy voice because it was considered cute or sexy. Breathiness, whether in men, women or children, is neither. If you have it, you won't be heard as well as those who speak with loudness and energy. You're likely to create a first impression of bewilderment, delicateness or conspiracy. Because breathiness is a sure sign of overly tense throat and neck muscles, you also may be opening yourself to vocal problems. This, fortunately, is easy to correct—simply project your voice. Cast or propel the sound forward, out toward your listeners; don't keep it bottled up inside.

• *Thinness* does not refer to the effects of dieting, but to a voice that seems to be produced from the lip of a balloon: pinched, childish, lacking in depth and resonance. It's difficult to convey power and authority if you have a weak, reed-like sound to your voice. As with breathiness, thinness is easily cured by speaking with more resonance, bigness and openness of tone. Try some relaxation exercises at the end of this chapter and work to open your mouth more to let the tone out.

• *Stridency.* Nothing turns people off more quickly than a shrill, shrieking voice. Such voices broadcast tension and nervousness, as do taut neck muscles and veins or the rigid posture that usually accompanies them. Caused by hypertension and insufficient breathing, a strident quality is sharp and metallic sounding with a high and squeaky pitch. Because stridency can lead to discomfort for you (and your listener) and unpleasant side effects (such as a sore throat and laryngitis), pay special attention to the relaxation exercises: yawn, roll your neck, massage your jaw. Note the old Quaker adage: "Head up, also chin; chest out, stomach in."

• *Harshness.* When you are angered, in conflict or feeling irritable, your voice may take on a rough, hard quality, often low-pitched. The first impression on strangers may be that you are an unsympathetic, sarcastic or overbearing person. If relaxation and breathing exercises don't get rid of this problem, don't take any chances—see a throat specialist. General treatment of benign vocal conditions may include nutritional changes, hot fluids, inhalation of steam, antibiotics, vocal rest and voice therapy. If untreated, or if these treatments don't work, you may need more serious medical attention.

• *Hoarseness.* If your voice develops a hoarse quality – a combination of harshness and breathiness – seek immediate medical attention, as the American Cancer Society recommends. While hoarseness may signal laryngitis and the onset of a cold, it may be a sign of more serious problems if it persists.

A colleague of mine developed a raspy hoarseness, which came on so gradually she didn't notice, especially because she had no pain or swallowing problem. Not wishing to alarm her, I pointed out the change and suggested she get a checkup. The physician found several nodules and scheduled her for immediate surgery. Fortunately, the nodules were benign. After surgery and four days of total silence, plus careful monitoring of her food and drink, she had her pear-shaped tones back.

If you are a cigarette smoker or heavy drinker, if you shout a lot or talk excessively in your work, or if you use a pitch above or below your normal level, you are vulnerable to voice problems. There's no question that cigarette smoking is directly related to cancer of the vocal cords. If you do smoke, don't speak while exhaling the smoke; that forces the smoke right across the vocal folds, which can be very irritating. And if you must work in polluted air, make every effort to obtain as fresh an air supply as possible.

In summary, voice quality gives both you and your listener subtle but clear evidence of how relaxed or tense you are. It reveals self-confidence or self-consciousness and even offers some clues as to how healthy you are. Recognizing your voice quality could save you from more than a poor first impression. It could save your life.

5. Sharpen your articulation. Articulation refers to the distinctness of the individual sounds you make. (It often is confused with "pronunciation," your choice of sounds to emphasize.) You articulate by directing the free flow of your airstream as you exhale. What would be a sigh or yawn becomes a syllable or word, thanks to the work of "articulators": your soft and hard palates, lower jaw, tongue, lips and teeth. The more carefully you use your articulators, the more clearly you will speak – and be heard. Good articulation has a range from informal to formal, depending on the particular setting. An interview or speech is a more formal setting than lunch with a colleague or a drink with the gang. In a formal setting, you make a better impression if you form sounds carefully and speak clearly.

Listen to yourself on tape. Do you hear words like "gonna," "didchwannta" or "Warshington"? Do your words run together? Are important sounds muffled? Are unimportant ones stressed?

If so, you're afflicted with the disease of "lazy lips," common to everyone from Jerry Falwell to Tip O'Neill. Sloppy diction can result in one or more of the following problems:

- *Substitution* – replacing one sound with another. Don't say "git" for "get," "jist" for "just" or "gonna" for "going to." I heard this from a TV evangelist: "the *since* of the world" (instead of "sins").
- *Addition* – adding sounds to words. "Ath-a-lete" instead of "athlete," "fil-um" instead of "film." I cringed when I heard a salesman urge me to buy a "bee-yoo-tee-ful" car. A Gerald Ford favorite was "judg-a-ment."
- *Omission* – leaving out a sound. "Suprise" instead of

"surprise," "nuclar" instead of "nuclear," "probbly" instead of "probably." And a favorite, this from a politician eulogizing one of his own: "He will live in immorality."

• *Reversal* – transposing sounds. "Interduce" instead of "introduce," "preform" instead of "perform," "modren" for "modern." If you need help, consider calling out the calvary.

The exercises at the end of this chapter can help you rid yourself of such problems. By practicing aloud and adjusting your speech pattern to fit the setting and context, you soon will master the art of speaking clearly.

Being clear doesn't mean being artificial. It means making sounds appropriate to your meaning and conveying the impression that you know what you are doing and that you are in control.

A strong voice is a valuable asset, an important corollary to confident and appropriate body language. It is essential that you match your nonverbal actions and your words with the way you speak, so the person meeting you for the first time hears a clear, confident and pleasant voice.

In Your Own Voice

Voice Warm-Up and Relaxation Exercises

We'll start with that tense body, and then work up to your voice box. These exercises also are terrific for overcoming jet lag, reducing stress and preparing yourself for more strenuous exercise.

Stretch – Make long, slow, lazy movements of your arms over your head, then bend and drop them, rag-doll fashion, toward the floor. Slowly swing your arms from side to side (don't bounce); come up slowly and stretch – first left side, then right; front, then back.

Make circles of various areas of your body – legs, hips, arms, torso. Start with small circles and make them increasingly bigger.

Relax your upper body, especially your shoulders and neck. Bring your shoulders up tightly to your ears and squeeze; then relax. Drop your head onto your chest, gently roll your neck back up, to the sides, then back down.

Concentrate on your face. Massage your lower jaw; stretch and relax your face muscles – mouth first, then nose and eyes. Make funny faces, stick out your tongue, wiggle your ears, scrunch up your nose. Have fun.

Open your lower jaw and say "ah." That sound will open your throat, force the air from your diaphragm and relax your neck, throat and tongue. Give a series of "ahs," each more forceful than the last. Notice how your pitch range has lowered.

Concentrate on your lips. Stretch them horizontally, purse them together, then let go; say "linoleum" out loud, over and over; hum the letter "m," keeping the sound forward so the inside of your upper lip becomes warm and tingles. That's proof you've learned to project the sound to the front of your mouth, where it should be.

Breathing Exercises

With your upper body and articulators relaxed, work on your air supply. These breathing exercises, done in sequence, can help relieve nervousness, stage fright, tension and stress. *Remember:* deep breathing replenishes your brain with fresh oxygen and, at the same time, takes away rancid carbon dioxide.

Yawn a big, rude yawn, taking in rich oxygen all the way down to the soles of your feet; now, very slowly, let the air out.

Sigh a deep sigh, letting everything, including your shoulders, slump toward the floor.

Pant, just like a puppy on a hot day, mouth open and tongue out. This exercise builds up your diaphragm and keeps your air canal open.

Inhale and exhale, deeply and slowly. Your stomach should move out when you inhale and your shoulders should not go up. When you exhale, your chest should not puff out. To test if you're breathing from the diaphragm, place your hands on your abdomen, fingers pointing together. As you inhale, push out against your hands with your lower ribs and abdomen. As you exhale slowly through your mouth, your abdomen should pull in. By breathing this way, you take all of the tension away from your larynx, while increasing the force you can bring to bear on a much larger source of air.

Articulation Exercises

- Make consonants (like d's, k's and b's) more precise, especially those at the ends of words.
- Sustain consonants you can hold—l, m, n, v and z—as

a way of shifting focus to the forward part of your mouth and away from the larynx. This also will allow you to slow down.

• Use a mirror to work on tongue and lip movement, using the following exercises:

Tongue

• Bring the tip of your tongue to a point.
• Bring your tongue out of your mouth without touching your lips or teeth.
• Move your tongue up and down rapidly.
• Draw circles with your tongue, clockwise and counterclockwise.
• Raise the tip of your tongue and dot the roof of your mouth, the edges of your upper front teeth and your lower teeth.
• Turn your tongue sideways, with one edge touching your upper teeth and one touching your lower teeth.
• Press your tongue against each cheek.
• Curl your tongue behind your upper and lower teeth.

Lips

• Round your lips, tensing and relaxing them.
• Purse your lips and smile – repeat rapidly.
• Build pressure behind your lips, and then explode the air.
• Raise your lower lip toward your nose, and lower your upper lip toward your chin.
• Smile with the right side of your lips, then the left side.

Chapter Four
What Do I SAY?

Chapter Four

What Do I SAY?

A joke among communication consultants goes something like this: two chimps were sunning themselves in their cage at the zoo when one turned and said to the other, "You know, humans sometimes look at each other, and occasionally make sounds with their mouths, but we have no solid evidence they actually communicate with each other."

To the contrary: those "looks" and "sounds" communicate more than ninety percent of the meaning in human interactions when people meet each other for the first time. It's the *words* they speak that don't contribute very much in the first few minutes – only about seven percent of the meaning, according to research.

How many times have you heard:

"I'm sorry, but I didn't get your name."
"Could you repeat that first item?"
"What was that point again? I was looking at your cuff links/listening to your accent/adjusting my hearing aid . . ."

Such remarks occur because the other person is too busy interpreting your nonverbal communication and analyzing the quality of your voice to pay much attention to what you're saying.

Don't misunderstand—words *are* important:

- A recent study by the American Management Association revealed that fourteen percent of a business executive's time is spent in telephone communication.
- People perceived as leaders talk more than others in conversations with both friends and strangers; more important, they stay involved in those conversations.[24]

Certainly the most effective communicator is one whose verbal skills are adapted to audience, situation and topic at hand, and one who presents a clear congruence among body language, voice and words. But your words become critical in relationship to the other, more dominant, channels of communication, especially during those key first two to four minutes.

When your body language and vocal attributes are appropriate and meet expectations, the viewer or listener can move quickly to the words you speak. At that point, your language should be powerful enough to sustain attention and contribute its share to the overall first impression. Words and phrases can be selected with that goal in mind. Even how you organize and support your ideas can add to the effectiveness of the impression you make.

Powerful language attracts others in much the same way powerful body language and voices do. Language also can work against you by detracting from your credibility or putting people off.

Consider the salesperson who poked her head into a businesswoman's office and asked, "Honey, is your boss in?" No "dress-for-success" clothing, no bright smile, no dulcet tone of voice could undo the damage of those first five words.

Or consider customers who complained to you because your receptionist called them by their first names.

Some employees follow through on your suggestions better when you start with a general conclusion and then move on to specifics. ("Randy, we're falling behind on project A. It might speed things up if you put the first draft on the word-processor instead of having Jim type it.") Some clients grasp your meaning more quickly when you bring along a model of the product and let them play with it. Others are persuaded more readily when you cite expert testimony. On the other hand, some don't want any examples, just a precise ticking off – one-two-three – of the salient features.

In each case, disparate though they seem, the choice of words or the arrangement of ideas may make the difference between a positive or negative impression, between understanding and action or misconception and disbelief.

As with your nonverbal and vocal communication, you have choices in how you select, arrange and support your words. This chapter focuses on three aspects of verbal communication:

- characteristics of "powerful" versus "powerless" language;
- patterns or arrangement of ideas; and
- selection of evidence to support those ideas.

Your answer to the question, "What do I SAY?" will tell you whether you use language to your advantage in making first impressions. When people get past what they see and hear to the words you use, are you ready to expand and exploit the seven percent that language contributes to initial communication? Your expertise, experience and knowledge, after all, lie not in your outward appearance but in your ideas as you convey them verbally.

To begin the process of understanding your language skills, you'll need to listen again to that taped sample of your voice from Chapter Three. If it's not handy, recall recent incidents or experiences where something you said seemed to make the difference – positively or negatively – or perhaps where something someone else said strongly affected you.

What's the Word?

We'll begin the discussion of word choice by identifying "powerless" language. There are four characteristics that may rob your language of strength and authority. Signs of such languages are *fillers, qualfiers* and *excluders*. Let's take them take them one at a time.

Fillers. Do you, uh, hear yourself "filling up" silences with, you know, words that mean nothing? Notice how, er, fillers detract from, well, the flow and rhythm, how they can, you see, distract or, umm, even irritate the listener.

Solve the problem by pausing when you feel a "filler" coming on. You don't need to fill the space with sound. Pauses can be powerful when used for emphasis, dramatic effect or just to give everyone time to catch up. Other tips for getting rid of fillers:

- Write each filler on several pieces of paper. Put a big red X through the word and post the papers in obvious places: on telephones, mirrors, pocket calculators, refrigerators and so on. Even place a miniature version on your watchband as a reminder.
- Get someone to nudge you or hold up a hand each time you use fillers.

These techniques can help you break the habit. You'll find the pauses you substitute (and eventually eliminate) will add to the effect. The rhythm will be restored and this niggling nuisance done away with.

Qualifiers are a second characteristic of powerless language and can damage your credibility more than fillers because they may undercut the very declaration you're trying to make.

Some qualifiers are called "hedges." They occur at the beginning of sentences and often precede the words "but" or "however": "You may not agree with me, but . . ." "I'm not certain this is correct, however . . ." "This may not be what you had in mind, but . . ." "I'm not sure, but . . ." "I don't know, but . . ." Such hedges tend to be spoken with nonassertive body language (such as downcast eyes, slumped posture or a nervous smile) and in a timid, uncertain voice. It's little wonder that power and authority evaporate, especially with people you don't know and who are trying to get a reading on you, say, at a meeting with clients or while negotiating a deal.

Another kind of qualifier occurs at the *ends* of sentences, as questions tacked on to declarations: "I'm correct, *aren't I?*" "Let's work together on this project, *shall we?*" "Harry is a good worker, *don't you think?*" Since tag questions require an upward inflection, a questioning tone is inserted at the exact spot a downward, positive one is needed. In one fell swoop you may have disavowed your assertive statement and chipped away at your credibility.

There are several ways to handle qualifiers. If the situation calls for a degree of tentativeness, fine, but try not to sound helpless or uncertain in all three communication channels. Don't, for example, drop your head, avert your eyes and ask your question in a timid, soft voice. You don't want the other person to mistake your uncertainty for passiveness. Whenever you can, simply eliminate hedges. Make the statement in a declarative or assertive manner and let it stand on its own.

Qualifiers at the ends of sentences serve little purpose.

When you want to ask a question, do so, but don't water down your statements by mixing the two. (An example: "Harry is a conscientious worker. Do you think he is doing a good job?") Practice dropping your pitch and inflecting down at the ends of sentences. Nip questions in the bud before they bloom.

Excluders. A third type of powerless language is that which excludes. People may forgive minor verbal sins of fillers and qualifiers when forming an impression, but chances are they won't if you alienate, stereotype or humiliate them, regardless of your intent. Just one word, phrase or sentence – even if said in an inoffensive tone with a sincere facial expression – may compel your listener to skip past these channels and focus on your language.

There is much greater power in language that *includes* people rather than excludes them, whether the setting is an office, courtroom, church, school or board room.

Say, for example, you call your staff together – men and women – to give them a pep talk. "O.K., you guys, our manpower is down because Harriet had surgery and might not be back for a while. You'll have to do yeoman's duty until the next salesman is on board. But I'm with you every step of the way."

What you have done is to exclude, and perhaps anger, your saleswomen (and sympathetic men). According to substantial evidence, people simply do not think of women when male-only references are used.[25] "Men," "his," "mankind," "manpower" and other such terms conjure up male images, whether the listener is male or female.

This is a touchy subject, as well it should be for those who are excluded. Gender-free, non-sexist language takes getting used to – not because it is awkward, but because it is a change from custom. Linguists assure us that, with minimal practice, we can use inclusive language as a matter of habit.

Here's a brief guide to alternative words and phrases. Tuck it in your briefcase, post a copy at your phone, hand it to those who look to you for guidance (or who you think need assistance):

- Avoid masculine gender pronouns. There often are ways to restructure sentences to avoid them. If necessary, use plural words like *they, people, staff* or *workers.*
- Use nonsexist expressions: *hand-made* or *synthetic* instead of *man-made; human resources, personnel* or *work force* instead of *manpower.*
- Employ nonsexist terms: *chair* or *chairperson* for *chairman; business owner, executive* or *manager* for *businessman.*
- Substitute nonsexist verbs: instead of *man the phones,* for example, try *staff, operate, cover* or *handle.*

Some rules of thumb to help guard against language that may offend:

- Use parallel words: *women/men, ladies/gentlemen, girls/boys, brothers/ sisters, gals/guys, wives/husbands* (*not* men and ladies, guys and girls and so on.) Avoid referring to adult women as *girls, gals* and *ladies.*
- Be parallel when using names. If it's "*Mr.* Gerdes" for him, it's "*Ms.* Gerdes" for her, not "Mary." If it's "Lynda" for her, it should be "Rollie" for him.
- If there are doctors in the house (M.D., Ph.D., D.D.S., or whatever), it's more equitable to introduce them in the same way you would other professionals: "This is Charlene DeHaven, my physician. And Jim Sack, my attorney. And my accountant, Amy Gilbert."
- Suffice to say, it is not powerful to call a woman *chick,*

girl, honey, babe or *sweetie.*
- Call other people by whatever name they offer when introducing themselves.
- Avoid reducing names to diminutive form. Don't change Debra to Debbie, for example, or James to Jim.

Just as sexist language excludes, so, too, does language that seems to be racist or suggests ignorance of another's culture. Consciously or unconsciously, it is tempting to fall back on stereotypes, on the presumed characteristics of a race, class or ethnic group. Remember that you are dealing with an individual and that by treating people according to a stereotype, you may unwittingly trigger the expected response – the self-fulfilling prophecy of the stereotype may cause that person to conform to your expectation.[26]

Inappropriate references to age also may be offensive and rob your language of its power. Why risk alienating clients, employees and younger people by calling them "kids," "boys," "girls" or "youngsters"? Choose neutral references. Similarly, it is wise to refrain from language that may offend those older than you – words like "honey," "dear," "old folks" or "people of the golden years." Try generic terms like "retired people," "volunteers" or "seniors."

Language that is highly technical or loaded with jargon also may exclude others and work against you in initial interactions. If you are dealing with lay people, avoid garbling your message with technical or legal terms, acronyms or "insider" talk. If your audience signals that more technical language is appropriate, you always can move in that direction. But it is difficult to undo the damage if your opening comments sound like a foreign tongue to the audience, or seem ostentatious or deliberately obtuse.

Finally, language that doesn't fit the situation will not be powerful: jokes when the context is serious, complicated sentence structure in informal discussion, chauvinist language in cross-cultural settings. These "misfits" will be spotted quickly and affect your image adversely.

I wish I could offer a universally accepted set of solutions to these problems. There is none, yet, although there are some excellent guidelines to inclusive language.[27] Until solutions emerge, why risk an interpretation that offends? Try to build in safeguards by avoiding words that might antagonize. If in doubt, ask those with whom you deal what they prefer. Call ahead to confirm the gender of an addressee. Ask what name the person prefers to be called. Better safe than sorry.

Language does play a powerful role in communication. The point is not to sanitize your vocabulary or to rob it of its uniqueness, but to emphasize the impact your choice of words has on others, especially during initial encounters. A careless remark that may hurt, anger or exclude someone is not worth the risk, especially because you may never know—by facial expression, tone of voice or verbal response—if you've been written off. And even if you know, it may be too late to change another's opinion of you, once you are judged to be unassertive, tentative, uncaring, ignorant or uninterested.

Powerful language, in contrast to powerless language, is:

- direct and assertive;
- free from qualifiers unless they're appropriate;
- devoid of disclaimers, hedges or apologies;
- simpler when spoken than written—more conversational in syntax, with fewer compound phrases;
- conversational in word choice—concise, animated, even fragmented; and
- brief and to the point—more is not better (consider the Twenty-Third Psalm or the Gettysburg Address).

Powerful language is *inclusive*. It brings people into conversation, regardless of their race, gender, ethnicity, age or disabilities. One need only to look at the sidetracked careers of politicians like James Watt or Earl Butz to understand the risks you take when you offend with words.

We Interrupt This Conversation. . .

One important characteristic of powerful speakers, in addition to their choice of words, is that they take their turns in conversations and prevent interruptions. This verbal skill helps establish and maintain credibility. There is a correlation between impressions of leadership and the ability to control conversations. According to linguists and speech-communication scholars:

- Men interrupt women much more frequently than they interrupt other men, and more often than women interrupt either men or other women.
- Men speak more often and at greater length than women, whether in male-only or male-female exchanges.
- Women don't take their turns as often or hold them as long as men.
- High-status males interrupt high-status females and low-status males and females; high-status females interrupt only low-status males and females.

For low-status individuals, the moral is to talk more often, hold your turn longer and prevent interruptions. This will cause others to perceive you more often as a leader.

Why are women interrupted more than men? Perhaps because women tend to have higher-pitched voices, thanks both to physiological differences and to the socialization of women to speak in higher and softer tones. Men tend to have deeper and louder voices, which allow them to prevail when they interrupt.

It may be that in conversations, people conform to the stereotype of the dominant male and the submissive female. New research suggests that verbally assertive females rate as favorably as males in communication competency.[28]

There is evidence that unclear or unassertive body language, regardless of gender, may be taken as cues from others that interruptions are okay. An intriguing study of British Prime Minister Margaret Thatcher illustrates why she was interrupted in Parliament more frequently even than men who ranked below her. Preceding most interruptions, she dropped her eyes, looked away or dropped her volume and paused.[29]

It may be that people with less power or position – men and women – use more fillers and qualifiers, which signal uncertainty or lack of preparation and may open the door for more assertive people to interrupt. More research is needed before we can be certain.

If you find you are frequently interrupted and want to do something about it, try some of the techniques listed below. Preventing interruptions, taking your turn and even interrupting others are important verbal skills. Try these techniques in the order listed. If one doesn't work, move on to the next.

- Don't look at the interrupter. If you do, you've effectively conceded and given up your turn.
- Continue making eye contact with the person you're talking to, even when interrupted. Raise your volume slightly and keep talking. In fairness, the other person may not have realized he or she was interrupting or that you wanted to finish your thought.
- Give a nonverbal signal you are not ready to be inter-

rupted. Hold up your hand up in a "stop-sign" gesture toward the interrupter, or reach out and gently pull the person into your conversation – all the time keeping eye contact.

- If none of the above works, try verbal cues: "I'm not finished. Wait a moment and you can have a turn." Or, "You interrupted at a bad time; just hang on a minute." Or: "When I finish this point, you're welcome to comment."
- Whatever you do, don't turn to the interrupter and apologize in a passive voice for being interrupted: "Please excuse me, but I was talking . . ."

At times it is important for you to interrupt others to take your turn or to make your point. Tips on turn-taking:

- To interrupt someone else, call that person by name: "Fran, I disagree with you." Most people like to hear their own name and will turn at its mere mention.
- Tag on at the end of someone else's sentence, or jump in where there's a pause. Have some stock transitions to smoothe the way: "That's an important point – let me add to it." Or "In addition to those factors, let's consider. . ." Then say whatever you want. With a reservoir of words or phrases you can interject yourself smoothly into conversation, gain or regain control and then add your two bits.
- Don't do conversational homework for others. Powerless people make all sorts of approving sounds and encouraging body language that just inspire the other person to keep on talking: sounds like *ummmm, hmmmmm, uh huh;* nonverbal cues like head nodding, smiling and lots of direct eye contact; and prodding questions or statements like *You think so?* or *Isn't that nice!*

Should power language always be used? Not necessarily. It is an alternative, a style to be familiar with so you can use it with ease when situations call for decisiveness and control. Just as you sometimes wear your "power suit" or assume a more powerful voice, so, too, should you have a power language you can choose to employ.

Occasionally, situations may require you to give an impression of acquiescence or compliance: a nurse following instructions from a physician, an employee responding to an irate boss or a traffic violator reacting to a police officer, for example. In such situations, you can adapt your words to accomplish an objective. But you do so because of *your* goals, and out of choice, not fear. Your choices are broad and deep. You don't have to be locked into one style or limited to one kind of vocabulary. That's why communication is such an unpredictable and exciting process.

What's the Big Idea?

Two other considerations about language are important if you want to make a good first impression: how to organize or pattern your ideas and how to support them. First, the verbal skill of organization.

People organize thoughts and process information in a specific fashion, based upon such factors as culture, education and how their brains tend to process information. Some may pattern ideas and data *inductively,* like the engineer who moves from specific information to a general conclusion. Others may organize material *deductively,* like the graphic artist who begins with a general concept or theme and then fills in the details.

The more you can learn about the other person's field of experience, the more accurately you can adjust and organize your ideas to fit his or her organizational approach and communication style. As the best salesperson I ever met once told me: "Find common ground right away. Find out their needs and wants. Then match those with the best you can offer by packaging what you have – your expertise, your product, your service – to appeal to the other person. Then close the deal."

That is excellent advice. It takes into account the tendency of people to want communication exchanges to have a beginning, a middle and an end. It recognizes that people remember little of what they hear, and that their attention span is so short it usually is measured in seconds.

If you don't present your ideas in what the other person perceives as a coherent, orderly sequence, you may give the impression you are ill-prepared, scatterbrained, disorganized or long-winded – even though what you say seems clear and well-organized to you.

Fortunately, some standard patterns of organization are adaptable to a variety of initial interactions: negotiations, interviews, public speeches, oral presentations, customer relations, telephone conversations and the like. I call these patterns "cookie cutters," because you can take the "dough" of the basic idea and press it out into all sorts of configurations, depending on the shape of the mold.

Here are seven "cookie cutters" and some suggestions for their use:

Numerical. Organize ideas in a 1, 2, 3 (or first, second, third) fashion. Great for action-type, high-energy people with short attention spans – as long as you don't go beyond two or three points. These people are bored with details and long-winded explanations. They want "just the facts, ma'am," as quickly and precisely as you can tick them off: "Ms. Valentine, three benefits of this health plan might interest you. The first is . . .the second is . . .and the third is . . ."

Chronological. Organize thoughts by time or history. Good for the process person, the one who wants structure, details, precision. "Mr. Lee, let me briefly review for you the background on this case beginning with our first intervention in 1965, and working our way to the present . . ."

Spatial. Organize ideas according to place or geography. Handy for both inductive or deductive types because it provides structure that can be broad or quite specific: "In planning your trip to Europe, do you want to concentrate on Scandinavia or the Mediterranean countries?"

Pro-Con. This pattern looks at an issue from both sides. It will appeal to "people people" – those who focus on human needs and concerns, not facts, actions or data. "Before we institute these new personnel policies, let's look at their impact on employee morale, as well as management goals."

Cause-Effect. This pattern moves from the reasons for, or causes of, an action to the specific effects or results. Going from *general* to *specific* may appeal to deductive listeners. For action types with short attention spans, use the reverse: Move from a *concise* listing of effects to *broad* probable causes. "The cause of acid rain is industrial pollution, and among its effects is the loss of fish life in Northern lakes. The rain can be traced to three areas . . ." (cause-effect) "Lack of productivity in American businesses shows up in poorly made products, decline in output and increased trade deficits. Among the many causes is the slow response of management to involve employees in decision-making processes."(effect-cause)

Topical. You can organize a subject or an issue into pieces or sections. This pattern might hold the attention of the "idea person," the dreamer who loves to take an idea and see how far it can go. "Ms. DeRoeck, can you tell me some ways industry can use dance and exercise to help reduce employee stress?"

Problem-Solution. This pattern organizes ideas in a straightforward fashion by identifying a problem and then stating or advocating solutions. This flexible pattern can be effective with nearly all styles as long as the focus is appropriate. People whose interests lie in data, for example, might respond to a quantitative statement of problem and solution. ("Let's examine the problem of costs when deciding on a new long-distance phone company.") Those with an interest in the human side of the equation would respond better to a pattern focusing on people. ("Will the new system improve communication within the company?") An action person might want to know the "bottom line." ("How much will it cost and when can we get it installed?")

There may be situations in which you haven't enough information or feedback to figure out the best pattern of organization. A good fall-back position is to apply the Rule of Three:

1. Tell 'em what you're going to tell 'em. ("Mr. Ochs, I'd like to talk to you about my company's new compensation package.")

2. Tell 'em. ("This package includes . . . and it is twelve percent less expensive than last year's for the same coverage.")

3. Tell 'em you told 'em. ("In short, this package gives you comprehensive coverage for just $2,550, saving you a lot of money.")

How will you know which pattern of organization to try, especially with people you've never met? Watch and listen for telltale signs during the first few minutes. Mentally check off such vocal and nonverbal characteristics as how fast they talk, how quickly they move and how often they change facial expressions. A fast-talking vice president, for example, isn't going to want to hear all the details a chronological explanation calls for, just a brief, concise outline. Maybe your supervisor is an amiable, slow-moving person who wants to hear all the details about why you need to hire a temporary assistant. If so, adjust your speaking pattern to match your supervisor's, perhaps by using a cause-effect pattern. By watching and listening, you can adjust your ideas and your style. It's a subtle but effective way of "fitting."

Supporting Roles

The more you learn early on about the other person, the more adroit you will be in employing the final verbal skill to be discussed in this chapter: choosing the supporting material to document your claim, amplify your points or entertain or inspire your listeners. This skill is especially valuable for those who must sell something, persuade others, manage conflict or serve other vital communication functions.

As with stock patterns of organization, there are different kinds of supporting material. Among them:

- facts, statistics, figures;
- examples, verbal illustrations;
- testimony – expert or personal;
- anecdotes, jokes, humorous sayings;
- imagery, analogies, comparison, contrasts; and
- visual aids.

Intellectually active people don't rely on mere skeletons of ideas – they flesh them out. And they adapt or tailor information to the fields of experience or communication style of others.

Think how pleased you were when the salesperson started telling you about the rpm, torque and mpg of the new car you were considering. She correctly perceived your desire to know about more than the color of the vinyl roof. Or how relieved your staff was when the new boss outlined the facts behind the consolidation and then went one step further to reassure them their jobs were safe. The boss anticipated and appreciated the anxious questions the staff would have. Recall how positively you viewed the job candidate when he gave a personal experience of past dealings with your company. These are savvy uses of supporting material that appeal to the people receiving the messages.

On the flip side, remember your irritation when the account executive wouldn't take "no" for an answer and kept snowing you with meaningless statistics. Or your frustration when a catalogue company ignored your expressions of dissatisfaction about a product and kept up a barrage of form letters with the theme, "Company policy is not to refund any money thirty days after receipt of the order." Recall your frustration with the person you met at a reception who kept dropping names and telling personal stories. Or how dismayed you were at the trainer in an all-day course who used no visual aids—not even a lousy flip chart or blackboard—but talked a mile a minute and expected people to keep up. In each case, consideration of the needs of the listeners might have turned a negative situation into a positive one.

When I talk about the many opportunities businesspeople have (or can create) to deliver oral presentations—sales presentations, employee orientations, board reports, speeches to community groups, media appearances and the like—I find busy people tend to shy away because they think they haven't the time for adequate preparation. My answer is that by making the time (either doing it yourself or assigning it to someone else) to keep up on appropriate topics, you will have a ready pool of supporting material from which to draw.

Here are five sure-fire ways to turn yawns into expressions of interest or even delight:

- Keep up to date on current events. Be a clipper, tearer and "highlighter" of newspapers, magazines and journals. Then work this topical information into conversations. Verbal repetition helps plant it in your brain for ready retrieval.

- Jot down insights or observations you make about work. These might include contributions made at meetings by you and others, quotes from clients and anecdotes and observations that lend interest, timeliness and relevance to your work.
- When using facts and figures in conversation, make them mean something in common, everyday terms. Instead of stating that verbal communication accounts for less than one-tenth of the message in initial interactions, for example, you might say the average person actually speaks for only ten minutes daily, or that the standard sentence takes only two and a half seconds.
- Where appropriate, use simple visual aids: photos, slides, models, cartoons, graphs, drawings, flow charts, maps and objects.
- Keep a card file of quotations, anecdotes, jokes and cartoons. Again, review them frequently and use them often – but only when appropriate.

You don't have to be an avid reader or a scholar to add such spice – just be the intelligent person you are who wants to be more interesting to others. You can do this by broadening the pool from which you draw information. To be interesting is to be listened to, and to be listened to not only is a mark of a successful first impression, it is one of the highest forms of power – especially in the world of business.

Words That Can Make A Difference

- Choose the name you use according to the kind of first impression you want to make. *Formal* names (Janet or James) suggest, according to research, people who are conscientious, emotionally stable, cultivated and less extroverted, as opposed to those with *familiar* (Jan or Jim) or *adolescent* (Janny or Jimmy) names.
- Work your name into the conversation again *after* the first two to four minutes have elapsed.
- Call other people by whatever name they offer when introducing themselves. Resist the temptation to use first names unless that is all they give out. Avoid reducing names to a diminutive form: don't change Ronald to Ron or Susan to Sue.
- Don't waste time by saying something important during the first few minutes. The other person is too busy "reading" you to listen. If you must utter words of wisdom right off the bat, repeat them later on.
- If you want people to skip over your appearance and voice to zero in on your words, say something unexpected or provocative – but be aware of the risks.
- Steer clear of loaded language or words that may trigger a negative response in people you don't know – words like *dear, honey, sweetie, mister,* for example.
- Check for feedback from other people right away, while they're too busy studying you to monitor their own response. Use that time and information to adjust your own body language, rate of speech and loudness levels, as well as the organization and supporting material of your ideas.
- When in doubt about your verbal response, remember that your words count for less than ten percent of the

meaning you convey during initial encounters. Pay attention to the other person with an appropriate style of listening, and let your self-confidence speak through what you look like and how you say what you choose to say.

Chapter Five
How Well Do I LISTEN?

Chapter Five

How Well Do I LISTEN?

A s a busy professional, more than half of your day is spent listening, and the percentage increases the higher you go on the corporate ladder. If you're a top executive, you may spend as much as eighty percent of your day listening — from that early morning breakfast with a client to an endless stream of meetings, conferences, luncheons, receptions and dinner parties.

The poor listening habits of Americans amount to a national scandal, costing millions of dollars each year in lost productivity and countless breakdowns in human relationships. Just how bad is our listening? Research shows:

- we use only about one-fourth of our listening capacity;
- we use only a tenth of our memory potential;
- we forget half of what we've heard within eight hours;
- eventually, we forget ninety-five percent of what we've heard, unless cued by something later on; and
- we distort what little we do remember.[30]

Successful companies realize the importance of listening. According to Thomas Peters and Robert Waterman, authors of *In Search of Excellence,* the managers of America's "best-run companies" build programs into their corporate communication systems to listen better to both customers and employees. The ability to listen, say Peters and Waterman, is the primary ingredient that separates excellent companies, both large and small, from their competitors.

As one wag wrote, we hear half of what is said, listen to half of what we hear, understand half of it, believe half of that and remember only half of that. If you translate those assumptions into an eight-hour workday, it means that:

- you spend about four hours in listening activities;
- you hear about two hours' worth;
- you actually listen to an hour's worth;
- you understand thirty minutes of that hour;
- you believe only fifteen minutes' worth; and
- you remember just under eight minutes' worth.

Eight minutes represents less than two percent of an eight-hour day.

All sorts of excuses and explanations have been offered for why we seem to be such poor listeners. Each explanation contains a kernel of truth. Here are my favorites:

- Humans have the attention span of a zucchini—less than forty-five seconds—after which our minds begin to wander and focus on other stimuli.
- We aren't formally taught listening as we're taught reading, writing and speaking, yet listening takes up more of our time than the other three skills combined.
- We think three to five times faster than we talk. As a result, we have a lot of thinking time to spare while listening to others—plenty of time to take mental coffee breaks.
- We filter what others say through all kinds of screens—cultural, racial, socioeconomic and others—so it is difficult to avoid distortion or bias while listening.

Fortunately, listening, like other communication skills, can be improved through effort and practice. You needn't take a course to learn how to become a better listener, although some good ones are available. You needn't even take a listening test, although some are available at little or no cost.

What you do need to improve your listening skills is a sense of how you listen, some motivation to improve and a few techniques to practice. That's what this chapter has to offer. So, as John Wayne used to say, "Listen up and listen good."

When people meet you for the first time, what kind of listener do they encounter? This is a critical question in creating good first impressions, because if you listen poorly, it may not matter how well you are dressed, how dulcet your tone of voice or how powerful your language. Poor listening can convey lack of interest, boredom, indifference or even hostility. Good listening has the power to draw people in and make them feel valued and understood.

To find out how attentive a listener you are, answer these eight questions:

1. Are you easily bored or distracted, especially if the person talking to you hasn't much power or isn't very attractive?

2. Do you listen only for facts or to evaluate, regardless of the type of message the other person is trying to relate?

3. Do you withhold feedback or response, perhaps by not looking at the talker or by maintaining a blank look?

4. Do you get impatient and interrupt others?

5. Do you focus on the other person's appearance or delivery, to the exclusion of content and ideas?

6. Do you focus on content to the exclusion of the person's delivery cues?

7. Do you let emotional language arouse, disturb or excite you?

8. Do you listen with "one ear" while mentally planning a rebuttal?

If you answered "yes" to one or more question, there's room for improvement. If you don't have an accurate or objective picture of yourself as a listener, see if you recognize any of your traits in the following dialogue:

> **Employee:** Hey, Sam, why did you give us some more stuff to type? We can't get any more time on the word-processor today, and we're already late on the work you gave us this morning. What do you think we are, superpeople?
>
> **Supervisor:** Look, Don, that's the instruction I got from upstairs. So get it out ASAP – we're really under the gun this week.
>
> **Employee:** Didn't you tell her we're running behind schedule as it is because the computer's been down so much?
>
> **Supervisor:** I don't make the rules and I don't tell the big bosses what to do. My job is to see that the work gets done and that's what I'm trying to do. You'll just have to work overtime or farm out some work to a temporary.
>
> **Employee:** The gang's not gonna like this.
>
> **Supervisor:** I'm not here to win a popularity contest. I'm here to do a job. Go work it out with them and get back to me.

Does that type of conversation sound familiar? Too often we have been at the receiving or sending end of such poor communication. Our experiences with poor listeners – the abrupt ticket agent, the bored hotel clerk, the impatient teacher, the hostile salesperson, the indifferent boss, the anxious secretary and on and on—are a source of continual irritation and frustration.

There's a pattern to the body language and tone of voice of these folks. Let's start with eye contact. Poor listeners usually look over your shoulder or to the side in search of someone or something more interesting. Their faces often have scowls pasted on them, or sometimes blank masks, but rarely genuine smiles.

Check out the rest of the poor listener's body language: arms crossed like a roadblock or hands on hips, with shoulders turned away. The poor listener taps fingers on a tabletop, checks out the clock on the wall, picks off imaginary lint.

Listen to a poor listener's voice. An occasional "uh-huh," "I see" or "hmmmm" is likely. So are interruptions intended to hurry you along. When poor listeners do speak, you often wonder if you're holding the same conversation. They often seem to ignore what you've just said and carry on with their own agendas. ("Reminds me of the time . . .") There's often a banality or cliche that indicates they really weren't listening ("We all have crosses to bear." Or "You could run it up the flagpole and see who salutes it.") Sometimes, they'll challenge the most insignificant details, ignoring the overall idea of the conversation.

Why are some people listened to and others not? There is a correlation between listening attentiveness and the authority the speaker may wield. People don't listen well to those they consider inferior, not very credible or unattractive. In their own defense, poor listeners may offer some of these reasons:

"They bore me."
"They don't look me in the eye when they speak."

"They say the same thing every time they open their mouths."

"They can't tell me anything I don't already know."

"They really don't want an answer; they just want to hear themselves talk."

"They take up too much of my time."

"They're never right."

"They always complain."

"They aren't interested in my troubles, just their own problems."

"They just need a warm body to talk to."

It's little wonder employees "go on and on" or bosses get anxious and impatient when talking to one another. It's not surprising customers get furious or salespeople frazzled. It should be no surprise mistakes are made, planes are missed, letters have to be retyped, orders reshipped, appointments rescheduled and meetings go on in perpetuity. That's the toll poor listening takes on people and organizations.

Ironically, good listening takes less time and is more efficient than poor listening. Moreover, it is more accurate and tends to leave both parties feeling better about their exchange. You needn't like other people to listen to them or to agree with what they're saying.

Let me describe three good listeners and traits they have in common.

I watched a well-dressed executive hard at work across the airplane aisle, his briefcase on top of the tray table. At a stopover in St. Louis, a casually dressed man boarded, took the seat next to the executive, pulled out a magazine and began to read. After the plane took off again, the two men discussed what each did; most of the conversation revolved around where the vacationer was headed and how good the fishing and tennis were there. The executive did not retrieve his briefcase until the plane landed. At that point, his seatmate handed the executive a business card and asked him to call in three weeks about an order he'd like to place.

His name was Les, he sat between us two women on a plane, and we learned we all worked in Washington. He asked interesting questions about what we did, how well we liked our work, what sort of problems businesswomen face and our concerns about the economy. He seemed genuinely interested in our answers, nodding and smiling. When the plane landed and we exchanged business cards, we learned that "Les" was Oregon Congressman Les AuCoin.

She's my car mechanic, founder of the Wrench Women, and she has more customers than she can handle. I assume it's not because she can fix anything on four wheels, but because before she writes up a work order, she gets her customers to give vivid and accurate descriptions of what's ailing their cars. She asks all sorts of questions: "Does it sound like this . . . ? Or like this . . .? Does it do that at 25 mph? At 45? At 55? Touch or point to the problem."

These people utilize three basic listening skills, coupled with some specific techniques. First, they adapt their styles of listening to fit the situation and the content of the message being conveyed. In addition, each makes some attempt to reduce environmental, cultural or interpersonal barriers that may hinder communication. And each is an active listener, watching for and giving feedback in all three channels – verbal, vocal and nonverbal. Within a few minutes, each brought a total stranger into a conversation, elicited a response, responded appropriately and established rapport – and a positive impression.

Expanding Listening Styles

Learning these skills and putting them together isn't difficult. The first step is to learn a style of listening that matches the type of message being conveyed. Poor listeners don't have this flexibility. They tend to respond with *their* dominant style, despite its inappropriateness in certain situations. Consider your lawyer friend who argues with everything you say. Or the boss who is so "laid-back" and nonchalant he wouldn't recognize problems if they danced up to him in a conga line. There's your former accountant, who listened only to the bottom line and never heard the nuances about what the business meant to you. And the physican who gives you the courtesy of a quick inquiry as to what ails you, while filling in your medical chart and interrupting you with rapid-fire questions.

Think of listening styles as falling along a continuum. At one end is a rather *passive* style, often appropriate when the other person simply needs you only to lend an ear – no advice, experience, assistance or even sympathy, just a minute or two to be heard. The listener need only give some quiet response – a nod, smile or occasional sound.

At the other end of the continuum is an *evaluative* style of listening, where the listener is expected to judge the merits of what is being said: good or bad, right or wrong, acceptable or unacceptable and so on. This style involves not just judgment and evaluation but an immediate and substantive response.

In between are two other listening styles. One is *social* listening, appropriate when meeting strangers at social events and professional gatherings or having ritual conversations with patients, customers or employees. Listeners who use this style are courteous, polite and pleasant – whether or not they feel like it.

The last listening style is *active* listening – a more comprehensive approach, involving listening with both eyes and ears – taking into account not just the words, but the way in which they are spoken. Active listening is characterized by active feedback through nodding, facial expressions, asking questions, paraphrasing and other means.

For the business executive I described earlier, who quickly and easily adapted a rather passive listening style appropriate to the needs of a vacationer, the payoff was a new client. Congressman AuCoin's active listening went beyond mere political courtesy; he probed, questioned, expressed interest – and we responded. My mechanic used an active listening style that approached the evaluative; she took in information, fine-tuning her questions until she had what seemed to be the answer to the problem at hand.

These people did what research makes clear is a fundamental technique in effective listening. They selected a style, usually more passive in the first few moments, and responded accordingly.[31] Then, as they gained more information about the nature of the message, the expectations of the speaker and the situation, they adjusted that style to best meet the situation. Sometimes, it involved sticking with the orignal style; at other times, it meant subtly shifting or blending styles. With such flexibility, these good listeners have enormous advantages over those who are locked into only one listening style.

Here are some strategies for expanding your listening styles:

Separate the person from the words. React to the ideas, not the person.

Find a need to listen. If nothing seems obvious, create a reason for listening. Even when you find nothing remotely valuable, or when you think it's beneath you to listen, remember that the other person *needs* to be listened to.

Be descriptive, not judgmental. Accept the good and bad aspects of delivery, content and appearance. Concentrate on helping the other person feel like a successful communicator. You may open the way to receiving useful, enlightening messages from someone you didn't like or respect.

Be flexible. Shift your listening style as the message shifts or as you get a better sense of the communication style of the other person.

Don't be "trigger-happy." Don't react to trigger words included in speakers' biases and attitudes. Keep your mind open and avoid overreacting, which has a detrimental effect on your ability to recall and process information accurately. Hold your fire and control your anger.

Overcoming Listening Barriers

Another characteristic common to the three good listeners described earlier is that they reduced barriers or interference that may impede or complicate the listening process. Some barriers are *environmental* (room temperature, seating arrangements, noise and lighting levels or interruptions). Some barriers are *interpersonal* (cultural differences, language problems, stress levels and verbal or nonverbal idiosyncracies, attitudes and expectations). Effective listeners employ a number of techniques to overcome such barriers. Some suggestions:

Pay heed to the environment. Attention spans are greater when there is sufficient air flow and comfortable temperature. Smoking reduces everyone's attention span, smokers and nonsmokers alike.

Sit with a purpose. The closer two people sit, the more carefully they tend to listen to each other. The farther apart people sit, the less effective their listening skills.

Don't chase butterflies. Concentrate and shut out distractions: close doors, put your phone on call-forward, go to a more private place. Resist the temptation to "switch channels" from the speaker to other stimuli, such as the attractive person next to you, your daily schedule or your unopened mail. Be mentally and physically prepared; if possible, think about the topic or situation in advance.

Cut out jargon. Respond with technical language only when appropriate. The better you are understood, the more you will be liked and respected.

Find common ground. As you listen, seek ways to identify with the speaker, but remain objective. Too much ego involvement will lower your comprehension; objectivity will heighten your ability to listen.

Reduce stress. The higher the stress level of either party, the shorter and less effective the listening level.

In the earlier examples, the business executive put his briefcase away and left it there. The mechanic talked in nontechnical terms, even making car-like sounds to elicit as precise a description as possible. The congressman made himself "one of us" and asked questions any businessperson might expect to hear.

How To Listen Actively

The final component of good listening is to listen actively. That means listening "between the lines" to changes in the speaker's tone, volume, emphasis, stress, voice quality and pitch. Good listeners watch not just the face and eyes but the more expressive lower half of the body, including hand gestures, body movement, use of touch and the way the person occupies space. Good listeners also give accurate and timely feedback – verbally and nonverbally – to the speaker. Here are other suggestions for listening actively:

Get physical. Get out of the office to where your employees and customers are. As you stop and listen to them, project your energy outward: look at them, make responsive sounds, swing your arms, cross your legs and so on.

Give something. Don't just take; communication is a two-way process. Give feedback in the form of head nodding, gesturing or questions.

Read people. Read nonverbal and vocal cues as well as verbal cues. Watch for "mixed messages" and what these might signal.

Fill in the blanks. Listen also for what is *not* said by filling in the gaps. Use the think-talk speed differential – our natural ability to process information four to five times faster than most people typically speak – to your full advantage. Concentrate on main ideas, summarize the content, anticipate what's to come and compare what's being said with what you already know.

Check and doublecheck. Rephrase in your own words what you think the message is. Again, summarize, paraphrase, repeat what you think you hear. Check the nonverbal with the verbal, the vocal with the nonverbal and so on. Take notes, both mentally and in writing. If you sense a discrepancy or if you're uncertain, ask questions.

The congressman looked at us, nodded, smiled and asked questions. The mechanic kept the focus on the car by pointing to or touching it, imitating its sounds and repeating what she heard. The business executive quickly read his vacation-bound seatmate and reacted in a low-key fashion that was right for the situation. All were active, involved listeners.

Underlying effective listening is the willingness to put aside personal biases and empathize with others, whether or not you like them or agree with them. That's what separates the mere "hearer" from the "listener." "Walk a mile in my moccasins," says an American Indian friend. "Feel the hard rocks of my life, the tender grass of my feelings; know the cold and damp spots of my life and experience the springy warmth of my pride and happiness. Listen . . . to me."

Empathy is evident in the following scene, where we see that a sensitive response reduces defensiveness and creates a postive climate that encourages problem-solving.

> **Employee:** Hey, Robin, why did you give us some more material to type when you know we can't get any more time on the word-processor today and we're already late on the work you gave us this morning? What do you think we are, superpeople?
>
> **Supervisor:** Sounds like you're really frustrated, Joel.
>
> **Employee:** I am. Not only can't we get enough time on the Wang, but the computer's been down again. Now this comes along.
>
> **Supervisor:** As if you didn't have enough to do before the end of the week, right?
>
> **Employee:** Yeah, I don't know what to tell the team about this.
>
> **Supevisor:** Would it help if I came down and talked to them?
>
> **Employee:** No, that's my job, but thanks for the offer.
>
> **Supervisor:** Well, get back to me about what you all will need to get the project done on time, and we'll take it from there.

Employee: Thanks, but with some rearrangement of schedules and delays on stuff that doesn't have top priority, we can probably get it done.

The supervisor attended to her employee's message, interpreted and understood it, evaluated it and then responded to it. She listened to both the content and the attitude being conveyed. As she listened – first reflecting and mirroring back – she switched gradually and appropriately to a comprehensive style. It is clear from their exchange that the two concentrated on each other's messages, not allowing distractions or interruptions to disrupt communication. Each was motivated to find a solution. Both, in fact, practiced good listening skills.

The benefits of good listening are both interpersonal and economic. People who feel they are listened to work cooperatively and tend to be better team players. They tend to perform better and have fewer on-the-job problems. As Sperry Corporation, which has the nation's largest and most comprehensive training program in listening skills, claims in its literature:

Good listeners think more broadly – because they hear and understand more facts and points of view. They make better innovators. Because listeners look at problems with fresh eyes, and combine what they learn in more unlikely ways, they are more apt to hit upon truly startling ideas. Ultimately, good listeners attune themselves more closely to where the world is going – and the products, talents and techniques it needs to get there.

Listening should not be our forgotten skill, for it is one

of the most important attributes of a professional. There is much power in being a good listener. There is the power to heal, to uplift and to make others feel valued and appreciated. And there is power in listening effectively to control interpersonal interactions. As Ralph G. Nichols, the grandfather of listening studies in this country, used to say, "Listening is an inside job—inside action on the part of the listener." That's the capacity to get inside other people and walk in their moccasins. It's the ability to listen with your eyes and your heart as well as your ears.

Chapter Six
Help Is On The Way

Chapter
Six

Help Is On The Way

*T*he "illiterates" of the next ten years won't be those who can't read or write, but those who can't learn, unlearn or relearn. The evidence is mounting. Studies collected by the Center for Management and Professional Development at Florida Atlantic University show that self-directed learning is both a necessary and desirable skill, and that success in a rapidly changing, high-tech world requires people who take more responsibility for their learning.[32] According to the Center:

> Today's successful manager can't spend valuable time in unproductive seminars that are sixty percent old stuff or sit around waiting for someone to offer just the right course. Nor can they expect much help from a mentor. The rapid rate of change rules out the existence of wise old heads to lead the way. Only those who can design their own learning can cope with that kind of constant change.[33]

This chapter is for you busy, assertive, independent people who want to take charge of the first impression you make—fine-tune it, improve a communication skill, rework your image. It's a guide for self-directed learning with three separate (but related) sections, each outlining a strategy and suggesting some materials, programs and resources to help you along the way. The strategies are:

1. Do it yourself.

2. Hire an expert.

3. Work with a group.

The approach – or combination of approaches – you select will depend on the time you have available, the amount of money you can spend, your own style of learning and whether you need the support of others.

Regardless of the strategy you select, promise yourself you'll take two crucial steps before doing anything else. First, conduct a "needs assessment" of yourself, based on what you've read so far in this book. Evaluate yourself – your dress, posture, voice quality and listening skills, for example – or, if necessary, hire professional help, such as a voice coach, image consultant or communication expert.

Second, set some objectives. Don't jump in feet first until you have decided specifically what you want to get out of your experience, set a schedule for achieving your goals and determine where, when and how you'll know you've achieved what you set out to do.

Now, stop your planning and get on with your strategy. When you've finished the project, evaluate what you've done, pat yourself on the back – and move on.

Here, in detail, are three strategies for self-directed improvement:

Strategy #1: Do It Yourself

Seeing yourself as others see you is critical if you are to work out a plan for improving your appearance or body language. Use this checklist to help set priorities:

Appearance Checklist

Characteristic	Strengths	Weaknesses	Action to Take
skin color			
gender			
age			
appearance			
facial expressions			
eye contact			
movement			
personal space			
touch			

To make a good assessment, you may want to use movie or video equipment to study how you sit, stand and move, and to evaluate your facial expressions and overall appearance. Alternatives are candid photos of yourself or a full-length mirror.

Whatever you decide needs to be done to make you look better, *do it*. Exercise, lose weight, buy a new wardrobe, sit up straight, practice facial expressions in front of a mirror, walk with more confidence, make more direct eye contact, whatever.

If you want to work on your *voice*, you first need to hear yourself as others do. Listen to voice samples – on an answering machine, dictation machine or any other tape recording – and critique all five characteristics as objectively as you can.

The only way to help yourself sound better is by practicing – out loud – and then listening to your progress and

Voice Checklist

Characteristic	Strengths	Weaknesses	Action to Take
rate			
pitch			
loudness			
quality			
articulation			

trying it again. Refer to the exercises in Chapter Three.

If you think your *language* needs changes, either in your choice of words or in the organization and support of your ideas, you can make improvements by following these steps:

- Listen to a recording of a telephone conversation or a recent dictation session. Make notes on how clearly your words flow, and on the sorts of evidence you used. Jot down any powerless language. (Refer to Chapter Four.)
- Next time you catch yourself using ineffective language, correct yourself on the spot.
- Make a list of words you tend to mispronounce or articulate poorly. Post the list where you can see it frequently. Occasionally read the list out loud.
- Make a list of words or phrases you use that might exclude or upset others. Study the list from the angle of the impression you may convey. (You may want to refer to *Without Bias: A Guidebook for Nondiscriminatory Communication,* available for $15.95 ($14.95 for members) from the International Association of Business Communicators, 870 Market Street, San Francisco, Calif. 94102.)
- Reread memos, letters or reports you've written (before your staff cleaned them up) and look for meandering

ideas, weak introductions, poorly supported concepts, inadequate transitions and ineffective conclusions.
• Try some of the suggestions in Chapter Four.

If you've decided to practice your *listening* skills, here are some things to do:

• Make a list of whom you listen to and whom you tend to tune out and determine how you can change that pattern.
• Listen to a variety of recorded material while you drive, walk, jog or sit. Many bookstores have audio tapes on a wide range of topics for managers and executives. Such tapes, usually featuring bestselling authors, also may be available at a local public or university library. Waldenbook stores have an excellent series of "Listen and Learn" cassettes on a variety of topics; write Waldentapes, P.O. Box 396, Old Greenwich, Conn. 06870, for a free catalog. Books on Tape also offers a selection of tapes for businesspeople; call 800-854-6758, toll-free, for a catalog.
• Send for the simple listening test designed by the Sperry Corporation for its employees. You can get a copy of Sperry's Listening Profile by writing to Department 4B, 1290 Avenue of the Americas, New York, N.Y. 10019.

In addition to these resources for working on specific characteristics, here are some general resources that shouldn't be overlooked as you seek to improve your first impression:

Public radio and television courses, produced in cooperation with local colleges and universities, sometimes deal with such topics as nonverbal communication, fashion, nutrition, public speaking and business writing. Check your local newspaper's TV and radio listings or write to National Public Radio, 2025 M Street, N.W., Washington, D.C. 20036; or Public Broadcasting Service, 475 L'Enfant Plaza, Washington, D.C. 20024.

Public lectures offered by educational or civic groups feature well-known or well-qualified people.

Training tapes and films deal with every communication-related topic. They can be rented for a modest fee (or purchased for a rather hefty one). Check with your training department for recent catalogs. One source is CRM McGraw-Hill, 110 15th Street, Del Mar, Calif. 92014.

Home study or extension courses include not just learning materials, but also feedback from an instructor. Costs vary considerably. For accredited schools and a list of courses, write to the National Home Study Council, 1601 18th Street, N.W., Washington, D.C. 20009, or check with a local college or university.

Finally, here are some little-known resources for free advice, information and assistance:

Department stores offer everything from fashion advisers and makeup consultants to seminars and speeches by experts and well-known authors.

Universities rely on volunteers to provide "real-world" exercises for student and faculty research. You may be the perfect guinea pig – and obtain free, expert help in the process, from hearing tests and tutoring for speech impediments to weight-loss counseling.

Libraries, including public and university libraries, offer all types of services: computer searches, listening booths for tapes and records, magazines and reference librarians who can solve amazing mysteries. I have been in public libraries throughout the United States at all hours of the day and evening and can attest to the use businesspeople and others make of them.

In brief, the "do-it-yourself" strategy requires a clear plan of action based on a realistic assessment of needs, a clear survey of resources and the willingness and tenacity to carry a plan through. You *can* do it yourself, but it takes motivation and practice.

Strategy #2: Hire an Expert

For rapid learning and personal attention and instruction, consider retaining the services of a professional. This may be a valuable investment in your future. Be advised, though, that such services can be costly. Moreover, there is virtually no accreditation process and it may be difficult to check qualifications and background. For these reasons, study the guidelines in this chapter *before* signing on the dotted line.

If you decide to go this route, keep in mind there are two distinct types of consultants: those who have been formally trained for work in the fields of image- and communication-consulting, and those who claim expertise through other means. For the sake of distinction, let's call the former *professionals* and the latter *practitioners*.

Professional consultants count among their credentials higher education, usually with advanced degrees, and considerable practical experience. As "experts" they likely have mastered a body of relevant knowledge. They continue their learning, either through professional organizations or additional training and accreditation. Many have published articles or books on their specialties. Further, they should, in my opinion, display membership in a recognized professional association (such as the Speech Communication Association; International Communication Association;

American Speech and Hearing Association; Society for Intercultural Training, Education and Research; American Society for Training and Development; or American Association of Business Communicators) and have a substantial client list (or a list of substantial clients). They often are associated with an institution of higher learning, either as a part-time or full-time faculty member.

It is this sort of person to whom you would look for training in nonverbal communication, voice improvement, public speaking, presentation skills and listening skills. The disciplines to which such people are attached – by virtue of education and professional association – tend to be speech communication, theater, vocal music, mass communications, English and audiology or speech pathology.

Practitioners tend to have no formal training, perhaps no advanced degrees and little involvement in professional societies or organizations. Their interest in a subject may stem from practical experience and their training may be limited to "certification courses" offered by franchises or entrepreneurs. These consultants tend to be found in the area of image awareness, fashion design and color consultation. Many are quite knowledgeable and can be helpful, but you will want to check their references carefully before investing large sums in their services.

The fact one consultant has an M.A. or Ph.D. is not a guarantee that he or she is a better teacher or more knowledgeable than another consultant with no advanced degree. One of the best consultants I know is an image enhancer with no college degree but impeccable practical experience in the fashion industry. She worked her way through the ranks of a large fashion magazine and then opened her own firm, where she now "dresses" many high-powered business and professional people who don't care a farthing about her schooling.

On the other hand, one of the least effective communication consultants I've ever encountered is an arrogant Ph.D. who has never left the ivory tower, flies his doctorate like a banner and doles out expensive advice on organizational communication to gullible businesspeople.

You probably want a person not only with expertise, but also with the skills, patience and good humor to help you make an effective first impression. Where to find such a person? Here are some suggestions:

- *Word of mouth* is still best. Ask a colleague or associate who has some experience of this kind to recommend someone. Talk to people in your training or personnel department who may work with such professionals. Word about who is effective tends to get around.
- *Articles* in newspapers, trade journals or newsletters by or about a consultant are worth following up on. Call or write the author. Then, having made contact, apply the criteria listed below.
- *Telephone* the head of the local chapter of the American Society of Training and Development and ask for references, or at least a list of prospects.
- Your *accountant or lawyer* may be able to recommend someone.
- Finally, and of least value, check *advertisements* in business journals, business sections of newspapers or your professional organization's newsletter. Note whether ads make reference to membership in a professional association or society. Don't rely on the yellow pages; many professionals avoid advertising there.

You've amassed a list of possible consultants, compiled a tentative plan of action and now are anxious to get on with it. You've set up an appointment with your candidate or arranged to talk by phone. What should you be looking for, listening for, trying to find out?

First and foremost, you should expect that person to make a good first impression. But that's just a start. You should assess each candidate's background and experience, approach to solving problems and the time and cost involved, as well as how each determines when goals and objectives have been achieved.

How To Select a Consultant. As you take in this information, weigh what you learn against the following questions:

- Does the consultant have graduate degrees or certification by a national association?
- Does the consultant have important clients, past and current?
- Does the consultant belong to professional organizations?
- Is the consultant's fee structure acceptable? (Depending on your particular needs and ability to pay, you may want to hire a consultant by the hour, for an entire project or on a retainer basis.)
- Does the consultant offer references and encourage you to check them?
- Will you work in comfortable surroundings?
- Is the necessary equipment provided, or does it cost extra?
- Do you like, trust and feel confident with this person?
- Does the consultant ask questions about your concerns, goals, schedules and the like?
- What's your "gut feeling?"

Some questions you should ask about payment:

- Is there a written agreement that includes both starting and stopping dates and that spells out the services, materials and length of sessions?
- Is there a charge for an initial consultation? (There shouldn't be.)
- Can you have an initial session before you decide upon a longer commitment?

Picking a consultant is not like buying groceries, for this person will affect your life in both subtle and direct ways. It is imperative there be a bond of trust and mutual respect from the beginning.

Strategy #3: Work With a Group

You may decide you want and need the experience and support of working with others. There are definite advantages: support for working toward a common goal, learning a lot in a relatively short period and often working under the supervision of a professional. There are disadvantages, too. You can't set your own pace and you must make compromises on schedules, commitment to completing the project and the content and methods used to meet your goals.

A little peer pressure never hurt anyone, though, and support from people undertaking the same project can be helpful. Besides, most communities provide a wide range of group interactions, as the following list – divided by probable cost – indicates.

Free or inexpensive activities:

- *Speech clubs,* especially Toastmasters and company-sponsored speakers bureaus, provide excellent opportunities to practice your public-speaking skills.

- *In-house programs* provided by nonprofit organizations as well as large and small companies offer training opportunities on a regular or as-needed basis. Consider seeking special help for you and your colleagues in public-speaking skills, selling techniques or telephone communication, for example. And if you work for a large company, contact the training department. It may be open to suggestions and would delight in your expression of interest.
- *Y's, parks and recreation departments and company programs* for physical exercise, including aerobics, swimming, dance and sports. By getting your body in shape you also may learn to breathe better, relax more readily, lose weight and tone your muscles, all of which help you feel better and project a more confident manner.
- *Community or readers' theater groups* are marvelous ways to get training and experience in everything from vocal exercises and movement to makeup and costumes. Even if it's just a walk-on part or a few lines, you'll learn stage presence – and have some fun.

Moderate-cost to expensive resources:

- *External training programs.* Many employers will pick up the tab for courses, seminars and the like – especially if they see value to the organization. Many employers also invest in workbooks, textbooks, films and other training materials. Provide your boss or training coordinator with information – cost, location, length of time, nature of the training and qualifications of the trainer.
- *Continuing education courses.* Investigate continuing education courses offered by local colleges and universities. They generally are reasonably priced and tax-

deductible. Taught by qualified people, they usually are scheduled in the evenings or on weekends. Many courses have no prerequisites. Their content is aimed at the working person rather than the college student. More to the point, taking such a course will keep you current on the latest research, get you back to books, put you on a schedule, hone your mind and give you a sense of accomplishment. You also may be granted access to campus resources, including gyms, pools, libraries and cultural events. Check especially these courses: oral interpretation of literature, voice improvement, public speaking, acting, debate and assertiveness training.

- *One-day seminars* sponsored by reputable community groups (chambers of commerce, business groups, service clubs, the American Society of Training and Development and the Junior League, to name a few). These will likely be conducted by experts, but keep in mind that the material will either be tailored to the concerns of the sponsors or will be very general to meet the needs of a cross-section of participants. Check the business section of your newspaper for information.

A word of caution about another sort of one- or two-day seminars. Between one thousand and three thousand professional suppliers offer thirty thousand to forty thousand separate courses and seminars in North America alone. They attract up to one million participants a year. *Caveat emptor* — let the buyer beware. Not only will the content, of necessity, be canned and very general (to interest a range of participants from accountants to zoologists), but the atmosphere will likely be a cramped room with poor ventilation. The ninety-five to five-hundred-dollar fee might be better spent in private consultation with a professional who knows your needs and concerns and can tailor solutions to meet them.

Audio tapes of these seminars actually may be more valuable than the seminars themselves. The sound quality will be better, there will be fewer interruptions and you can work at your own speed in a more conducive atmosphere — your home or office. Moreover, the workbooks and other course materials usually are clearer and better developed than the presentation.

Which leads to a final warning: before you plunk down that nonrefundable pre-registration fee, make certain the "biggie" pictured on the brochure actually will teach the seminar. Chances are a junior associate will.

With careful screening, however, seminars can provide you with valuable information. If you're interested, it means plowing through brochures, course catalogues and trade publications to find one worth attending.

One valuable guide is *The Seminar Market,* a comprehensive listing of more than thirteen hundred organizations offering seminars. This $70 directory is compiled and published by Schrello Associates, Long Beach, California. You probably can convince your company that purchase of the book is worthwhile.

Because there are so many fly-by-night operations in the seminar business, ask for references from several people who have taken the course you're interested in. Reputable seminar organizations supply references willingly.

A Final Note

You now have three strategies for learning new behaviors and unlearning old habits. Pick one strategy or a combination of all three, depending on your time constraints, level of motivation and access to this cornucopia of resources. As I've stressed throughout this book, you *can* tailor your first impression and modify unproductive behavior – that's the beauty, reward and power of self-directed learning.

Armed with these weapons of effective communication for a variety of encounters, you should be raring to put them to work. But even if you're frustrated with a lack of time, unclear as to where to begin or discouraged with your answers to those four key questions, my final advice is the same as that a flight instructor once gave a student pilot as the plane plunged nose-first toward the ground: "Do something, anything," said the instructor. "But do it *now!*"

A Sample Plan of Action

1. My primary need is to improve my listening skills.

2. My goal is to learn several styles of listening.

3. My objectives:

    a. measure current listening skills;

    b. check with others as to my listening abilities;

    c. spend a half-hour per day in listening/retention activities; and

    d. measure my progress at end of four-week period.

4. My survey of available resources includes:

    a. tapes on listening that can be borrowed from a listening association;

    b. university's walk-in clinic that will measure my hearing;

    c. training department at work that thinks a short course on listening can be added to its list of offerings;

    d. several reputable firms in area that can administer listening tests;

    e. the Sperry Listening Profile; and

    f. friends and spouse who are willing to give me periodic feedback on my progress.

5. My only supplies to be purchased are a tape recorder and some blank cassettes. I will work one-half hour before work in my office to ensure privacy and quiet.

6. My means of evaluation will be to have my hearing checked, to take a listening retention test every three weeks and to check with trusted friends and colleagues as to whether they've noted improvement.

7. The strategy I chose is a combination of self-help and professional assistance. I will especially utilize experts from the university's speech and hearing clinic. I will push for an internal training course at work and until that is in place will try to get company authorization to attend an extension course on listening skills offered by the community college.

8. My schedule for all of the above is as follows:

Week One
- begin listening tests
- write International Listening Association
- make appointment at university clinic
- check with training department
- check on external training possibilities

Week Two
- get hearing tested
- take listening tests
- with test results, set goals and objectives
- practice active listening skills
- start half-hour-per-day listening exercises

Week Three
- get feedback from others
- continue half-hour per day on retention skills

Week Four
- try different listening styles
- take retention test
- check response of others
- continue half-hour exercises

Notes

CHAPTER ONE

1. Leonard Zunin and Natalie Zunin, *Contact: The First Four Minutes* (New York: Ballantine Books, 1972). The Zunins arrived at this figure from their studies of hundreds of people in dozens of settings.

2. Martha Rader and L.P. Wunsch, "A Survey of Communication Practices of Business School Graduates by Job Category and Undergraduate Majors," *The Journal of Business Communication,* Summer 1980, p. 35.

3. The study was conducted by Communispond, Inc., and reported in *Training/Human Resource Development,* October 1981, pp. 19-20.

4. See Albert Mehrabian, *Nonverbal Communication* (Chicago: Aldine-Atherton, 1972); Erving Goffman, *Encounters: Two Studies in the Sociology of Interaction* (Indianapolis and New York: Bobbs-Merrill, 1961); William C. Donaghy, "Our Silent Language," in *Components in Communication* (Dubuque, Iowa: Gorsuch Scarisbrick, 1976); D.H. Zimmerman and C. West, "Sex Roles, Interruptions and Silences in Conversations," in *Language and Sex: Differences and Dominance,* Barrie Thorne and Nancy Henley, eds., (Rowley, Mass.: Newbury House, 1975); and Ray L. Birdwhistell, *Kinesics and Context* (Philadelphia: University of Pennsylvania Press, 1970).

5. Mehrabian, *Silent Messages,* 2nd ed. (Belmont, Calif.: Wadsworth Publishing, 1982); Mehrabian and Susan Ferris, "Interference of Attitudes from Nonverbal Communication in Two Channels," *Journal of Consulting Psychology* 31, 1967, pp. 248-52; and Birdwhistell, "Paralanguage: Twenty-five Years After Sapir" (unpublished manuscript, 1959), cited by T.G. Hegstrom, "Message Impact: What Percentage Is Nonverbal?" *Western Journal of Speech Communication* 13, Spring 1979, pp. 134-42.

6. Nancy Henley, *Body Politics, Power, Sex and Nonverbal Communication* (Englewood Cliffs, N.J.: Prentice-Hall, 1977).

7. Mark Snyder, "Self-Fulfilling Stereotypes," *Psychology Today*, July 1982, pp. 60-68.

8. Beth Ann Krier, "The Tell-Tale Voice: Expert's Window on the Personality," *Los Angeles Times*, November 3, 1982, Part V, pp. 1, 7; and *Brain and Mind Bulletin*, January 25, 1983, pp. 1-2.

9. Ronald S. Miller, "The Voice System: Foundation for a New Psychology" (unpublished manuscript, 1982, describing Sandra Seagal's work).

10. Excellent review by Robert Rosenthal and Bella M. De Paulo, "Expectancies, Discrepancies, and Courtesies in Nonverbal Communication," *Western Journal of Speech Communication*, Spring 1979, pp. 76-95; and Mehrabian, *Nonverbal Communication*, pp. 179-90.

CHAPTER TWO

11. See list of recommended readings, page 145.

12. M.G. Efran, "The Effect of Physical Appearance on the Judgment of Guilt, Interpersonal Attraction and Severity of Recommended Punishment in a Simulated Jury Task," *Journal of Experimental Research in Personality* 8 (1974), pp. 45-54; and E.N. Solender and E. Solender, "Minimizing the Effect of the Unattractive Client on the Jury," *Human Rights* 5 (1976), pp. 201-14.

13. E. Berscheid and E. Walster, "Physical Attractiveness," in L. Berkowitz, ed., *Advances in Experimental and Social Psychology* 7 (1974), pp. 158-215; and W. Goldman and P. Lewis, "Good-Looking People Are Likable, Too!" *Psychology Today*, July 1977, p. 27.

14. Mark Knapp, *The Essentials of Nonverbal Communication* (New York: Holt, Rinehart and Winston, 1980), pp. 108-09;

Donaghy, *Components in Communication,* p. 25; and Snyder, *Psychology Today,* pp. 60-68.

15. Barbara Eakins and R. Gene Eakins, *Sex Differences in Human Communication* (Boston: Houghton Mifflin Co., 1978); Cheris Kramarae, *Women and Men Speaking* (Rowley, Mass.: Newbury House, 1981); and Marianne La France and Clara Mayo, "A Review of Nonverbal Behaviors of Women and Men," *Western Journal of Speech Communication,* pp. 96-107.

16. Susan Sontag, "The Double Standard of Aging," *Saturday Review,* September 23, 1972, pp. 29-38.

17. Paul Ekman, Robert Levenston, and Wallace Friesen, "Autonomic Nervous Activity Distinguishes Among Emotions," *Science* 221 (September 1983), pp. 1,208-10.

18. Paul Ekman and Wallace Friesen, *Unmasking the Face* (Englewood Cliffs, N.J.: Prentice-Hall, 1975).

19. Study by psychologists Betty Grason (Hofstra University) and Morris Stein (New York University), reported in "Newsline," *Psychology Today,* August 1980, p. 20.

20. J.K. Burgoon and S.B. Jones, "Toward a Theory of Personal Space Expectations and Their Violation," *Human Communication Research* 2 (1976), pp. 131-46; Edward T. Hall, *The Silent Language* (Garden City, N.Y.: Doubleday, 1959); and Nan M. Sussman and Howard K. Rosenfeld, "Influence of Culture, Language and Sex on Conversational Distance," *Journal of Personality and Social Psychology* 42 (1982), pp. 66-74.

CHAPTER THREE

21. Paul G. Friedman, *Listening Processes: Attention, Understanding, Evaluation* (Washington, D.C.: National Education Association, 1978), pp. 23-27; and Ralph R. Nichols, "Listening Is a Ten-Part Skill," *Nation's Business* 45 (July 1957), p. 56.

22. James MacLachen, "What People Really Think of Fast Talkers," *Psychology Today*, November 1979, pp. 113-17.

23. D.W. Addington, "The Relationship of Selected Vocal Characteristics to Personality Perception," *Speech Monographs* 35 (1968), pp. 492-503; J.R. Davitz, *The Communication of Emotional Meaning* (New York: McGraw-Hill, 1964); and J.D. Moe, "Listener Judgments of Status Cues in Speech: A Replication and Extension," *Speech Monographs* 39 (1972), pp. 144-47.

CHAPTER FOUR

24. Study by sociologist Paul A. Reynolds, University of Minnesota, reported in "Newsline," *Psychology Today*, November 1980, p. 28.

25. Two thorough reviews of the data are Cheris Kramer, Barrie Thorne, and Nancy Henley, "Perspectives on Language and Communication," *Signs* 3 (1978), pp. 638-51; and Wendy Martyna, "Beyond the 'He/Man' Approach: The Case for Nonsexist Language," *Signs* 5 (1980), pp. 482-93.

26. Snyder, *Psychology Today*, pp. 60-68.

27. Casey Miller and Kate Swift, *The Handbook of Nonsexist Writings: For Writers, Editors and Speakers* (New York: Lippincott and Crowell, 1980); and *Guidelines for Equal Treatment of the Sexes* (New York: McGraw-Hill, 1974).

28. Johnny T. Murdock and Catherine W. Konsky, "An Investigation of Verbosity and Sex-Role Expectations," *Women's Studies in Communication* 5 (Fall 1982), pp. 65-76.

29. "Invited Interruptions," *Discover*, March 1983, pp. 15-18. (A summary of the work of Geoffrey Beattie and colleagues.)

CHAPTER FIVE

30. Larry Barker, *Listening Behavior* (Englewood Cliffs, N.J.: Prentice-Hall, 1971); and Nichols, *Nation's Business*, p. 57.

31. Barker, *Listening Behavior;* Friedman, *Listening Processes;* Nichols and Leonard Stevens, "Listening to People," *Harvard Business Review* 35 (January-February 1957), pp. 85-92; and Andrew D. Wolvin and Carolyn G. Coakley, *Listening* (Dubuque, Iowa: Wm. C. Brown, 1982).

CHAPTER SIX

32. Ron Zemke, "Self-Directed Learning: A Must Skill in the Information Age," *Training/HRD*, August 1982, pp. 28-32.

33. Zemke, "Self-Directed Learning," p. 28.

Suggested Readings

Argyle, Michael. *Social Interaction.* New York: Atherton Press, 1969.

Barker, Larry. *Listening Behavior.* Englewood Cliffs, N.J.: Prentice-Hall, 1971.

Birdwhistell, Ray L. *Kinesics and Context.* Philadelphia: University of Pennsylvania Press, 1970.

Cho, Emily, and Lueders, Hermine. *Looking, Working, Living Terrific Twenty-four Hours a Day.* New York: G.P. Putnam's Sons, 1982.

Eakins, Barbara, and Eakins, R. Gene. *Sex Differences in Human Communication.* Boston: Houghton Mifflin Co., 1978.

Ekman, Paul, and Friesen, Wallace. *Unmasking the Face.* Englewood Cliffs, N.J.: Prentice-Hall, 1975.

Goffman, Erving. *Encounters: Two Studies in the Sociology of Interaction.* Indianapolis and New York: Bobbs-Merrill, 1961.

Hall, Edward T. *Beyond Culture.* New York: Doubleday & Co., 1976.

Hall, Edward T. *The Hidden Dimension.* New York: Anchor Press/Doubleday, 1969.

Hanley, Theodore D. and Thurman, Wayne L. *Developing Vocal Skills.* New York: Holt, Rinehart & Winston, 1970.

Henley, Nancy M. *Body Politics: Power, Sex and Nonverbal Communication.* Englewood Cliffs, N.J.: Prentice-Hall, 1977.

Kleinke, Chris. *First Impressions: The Psychology of Encountering Others.* Englewood Cliffs, N.J.: Prentice-Hall, 1975.

Knapp, Mark L. *Nonverbal Communication in Human Interaction.* 2nd ed. New York: Holt, Rinehart & Winston, 1978.

Lakoff, Robin. *Language and Woman's Place.* New York: Harper Colophon Books, 1975.

Malandro, Loretta A. and Barker, Larry. *Nonverbal Communication.* Reading, Mass.: Addison-Wesley, 1983.

Mehrabian, Albert. *Nonverbal Communication.* Chicago: Aldine-Atherton, 1972.

Mehrabian, Albert. *Silent Messages,* 2nd ed. Belmont, Calif.: Wadsworth Publishing Company, 1982.

Miller, Casey, and Swift, Kate. *Words and Women: New Language in New Times.* New York: Doubleday & Co., 1975.

Molloy, John T. *Dress for Success.* New York: Warner Books, 1976.

Morrisey, George L. *Effective Business and Technical Presentations,* 2nd ed. Reading, Mass.: Addison-Wesley, 1982.

O'Connell, Sandra E. *The Manager as Communicator.* New York: Harper & Row, 1979.

Peters, Thomas J., and Waterman, Robert H. Jr. *In Search of Excellence: Lessons from America's Best-Run Companies.* New York: Harper & Row, 1982.

Steil, Hyman K.; Barker, Larry L; and Watson, Kattie W. *Effective Listening.* Reading, Mass.: Addison-Wesley, 1983.

Stone, Janet, and Bachner, Jane. *Speaking Up.* New York: McGraw-Hill, 1977.

Thorne, Barrie, and Henley, Nancy, eds. *Language and Sex: Difference and Dominance.* Rowley, Mass: Newbury House, 1975.

Uris, Dorothy. *A Woman's Voice: A Handbook To Successful Private and Public Speaking.* New York: Barnes Noble Books, 1975.

Wolvin, Andrew D., and Coakley, Carolyn Gwynn. *Listening.* Dubuque, Iowa: Wm. C. Brown, 1982.

Zunin, Leonard, M.D., and Zunin, Natalie. *Contact: The First Four Minutes.* New York: Ballantine Books, 1972.

Index

JANET G. ELSEA, PH.D., is founder and president of Communications Skills, Inc., a Washington, D.C., consulting firm with an office in Tucson, Arizona. Communications Skills, Inc., designs and implements training programs, seminars and workshops tailored to the needs of clients. Topics include effective speaking and writing, organizational communication, management and leadership training, assertive communication, conflict and stress management and performance appraisal. Clients have included The World Bank, Georgetown University Law Center, the Corporation for Public Broadcasting, the Carter White House, Valley National Bank of Arizona, Honeywell, Inc. and The Smithsonian Institution.

Dr. Elsea received her Ph.D. from the University of Iowa in speech communication and theater; her M.A. and B.A. degrees are from the University of California at Davis. Between 1970 and 1978, she was a professor of communication at Arizona State University, serving one term as its division chair. She has been a visiting professor of communication at American University in Washington, D.C., a visiting scholar at the West Coast Cancer Foundation in San Francisco, and a lecturer at the University of Massachusetts in Amherst.